SACRED DANCE

SACRED DANCE

Encounter with the Gods

MARIA-GABRIELE WOSIEN

THAMES AND HUDSON

ART AND IMAGINATION
General Editor: Jill Purce

Published in the United States in 1986 by
Thames and Hudson Inc., 500 Fifth Avenue,
New York, New York 10110

Library of Congress Catalog Card Number 85-52298

Printed and bound in Spain by Artes Graficas Toldeo S.A.
D.L TO–1891–85

Contents

ACKNOWLEDGMENTS

Objects in the plates are reproduced by courtesy of the following:
American Museum of Natural History, New York 59
National Museum, Athens 33
Kurt Bachmann 31
Bibliothèque Nationale, Paris 56
Bodleian Library, Oxford 29
British Museum, London 8, 9, 12, 30, 43, 53
Brooklyn Museum 14
Cairo Museum 15, 25
Chester Beatty Library, Dublin 40
Published by permission of the Director of Antiquities and
Cyprus Museum 2
Ferdinandeum, Innsbruck 48
Musée Guimet, Paris 10
India Office Library, London 22
Louvre, Paris 7, 47
Instituto Nacional de Antropología e Historia, Mexico 18
Ajit Mookerjee 26
Museo Nazionale, Naples 27, 36
National Gallery, London 19
Museo Nazionale, Palermo 21
Pierpont Morgan Library, New York 39
Museo di San Marco, Florence 20
Dr Kurt Stavenhagen 37
Stendahl Galleries 38
Museo Nazionale, Taranto 42
Museo Nazionale, Tarquinia 23
Topkapi Museum, Instanbul 46
Victoria and Albert Museum, London 11, 16, 24
Mrs N. V. Williams 4
Worcester Art Museum 6

Photographs are by the following:
Alinari 1, 21, 50; figs. 12, 56, 57, 66
Courtesy of the Museum of the American Indian.
Heye Foundation fig. 48
Courtesy of American Museum of Natural History fig. 39

Ferdinand Anton 34
Archives Photographiques fig. 65
Ardea Photographics (Åke Lindau) 52
Australian Information Service 55, 58; fig. 24, 37, 61, 74
Courtesy of the Byzantine Institute Inc. fig. 2
Camera Press 3, 51, 60; fig. 55
Department of the Environment. Crown Copyright fig. 5
Deutsches Archäologisches Institut, Athens 33; fig. 46
Deutsches Archäologisches Institut, Rome fig. 67
R. Edwards fig. 75
Alfredo Foglia 28
Giraudon 7, 10
The John Hillelson Agency Ltd (Marilyn Silverstone) 13;
(Bruno Barbey) 54
Hirmer Fotoarchiv 35; figs. 6, 13, 29, 32
International Society for Educational Information, Tokyo,
Inc. 17; fig. 44
Shuhei Iwamoto 57
Jean-Dominique Lajoux 41
Richard Lannoy 44
Professor A. Maiuri fig. 62
Mansell fig. 25, 35, 43, 52, 54, 63, 72
Mansell-Brogi fig. 58
Metropolitan Museum of Art, New York fig. 76
National Film Archive fig. 38
Oriental Institute of Chicago fig. 69
Dr Cornelius Ouwehand fig. 20
Picturepoint 32
Paul Popper Ltd 52; figs. 8, 21, 22, 47, 51
Josephine Powell fig. 27
Radio Times Hulton Picture Library fig. 14, 30
Ronan Picture Library and E. P. Goldschmidt and Co. Ltd
fig. 80
Sangeet Natak Akademi, New Delhi 45; fig. 28
Scala 20, 23, 27, 36
Jeff Teasdale 26
Eileen Tweedy 11, 16, 24, 49

Encounter with the gods

That suffering also
which I showed to thee and the rest
in the dance,
I will that it be called a mystery.

('Hymn of Jesus', Acts of St John.)

Cosmos and man

When the mind inquires into the existence of the world, it answers itself in terms of causality, quoting a primary cause. The myths of man speak of the creation of the world as the dance of God. Shiva Nataraja, Lord of the Dance, sends pulsating waves of awakening sound through matter, thereby seducing it to life from lethargy. And matter dances, appearing round about him as an aureole of fiery emanations. Dancing, he creates and sustains the manifold phenomena of the universe; dancing he destroys by fire all forms and names and gives new rest:

His form is everywhere, all pervading. . . .
Everywhere is Shiva's gracious dance made manifest. . . .
He dances with Water, Fire, Wind and Ether.
Thus our Lord dances ever in the court.

The creator is seen as the 'unmoved mover' behind events in the cosmos, the still point round which everything must turn, simply because it holds its peace, encompassing both movement and perfect immobility. Rhythmic sound, in cosmogonic myths, is at the root of all creation; and the gods are – or God is – the formulated power through which the life-force manifests itself. Truth, being beyond sound and rhythm, is the invisible divine centre round which all creation dances.

The Roman second-century poet Lucian sees the dance as the beginning of creation: 'With the creation of the universe the dance too came into being, which signifies the union of the elements. The round dance of the stars, the constellation of planets in relation to the fixed stars, the beautiful order and harmony in all its movements, is a mirror of the original dance at the time of creation. The dance is the richest gift of the muses to man. Because of its divine origin it has a place in the mysteries and is beloved by the gods and carried out by men in their honour' (On the Dance).

The whole of existence is woven into the cycle of becoming, stretching between birth and death, experiencing ascent and decline; and life, when it has clothed itself for a while with sounds, gestures, forms, when it has ruled a while in manifestation, returns in silence to its own slumber. Birth, life, death, and new birth, as an unending cycle, set the permanent stage for the manifold processes and phenomena of existence.

In a creation legend of the Jicarilla Apache Indians, the creator fashioned a bird from mud and whirled it round. This movement caused the emanation of 'dream-like forms'; the bird grew dizzy, and, as one does when dizzy, it saw images round about.

Dazed, man awoke from his dreams in a world which he could not understand, the mystery of which inspired him with wonder and fear that made him strive to fathom its depths. Everywhere and at all times, man has been confronted with the manifestation of a power beyond himself: in nature, in the sky, during growth, at birth, illness and death. The times of crisis, calling into question man's life in relation to the world, attract like magnets; they provide an experience of threshold, by confronting man with his limitations. And yet power also often reveals itself in some wholly unexpected manner, thus turning life into a dangerous affair, full of critical moments.

Faced with the chaos of experience and with his own powerlessness, man felt the need to transcend his condition, for his life depended on his ability to establish a lasting bond with the source of power, and to apprehend the laws governing its manifestation. Life was experienced as constant movement, linked by a universal sympathy with all phenomena through one uniting force. Plants, animals, stars and men were bound together in a single stream, with the possibility of always transforming themselves one into the other. This state where everything participates with everything else, the merging of forms, lives on in us in the fabric of our dreams and nostalgias. The dance was man's natural way of attuning himself to the powers of the cosmos. Rhythmic movement provided the key for both creating and reintegrating the 'dream-like forms', and was thus a means of being in touch with the source of life.

Dance, as an expression of man being moved by the transcendent power, is also the earliest art form; before man expresses his experience of life through materials he does so with his own body. Early man dances on every occasion: for joy, grief, love, fear;

at sunrise, death, birth. The movement of the dance provides him with a deepening of his experience. In his dancing, the imitation of sound and movement observed around him, and especially the involuntary expression of motion through sound and gestures, precedes any consciously articulated sound and dance formation. Before the dance develops into a deliberate religious rite, it is a rhythmic release of energy, an ecstatic act. Only very gradually, under the influence of established cults, is the dance transformed from a spontaneous expression of movement to a fixed pattern of steps, gestures and poses. Yet, in whatever form the dance presents itself, it always aims at approaching the god. As an act of sacrifice, as man giving himself to his god, the dance is total surrender.

In this way the body, in the whole range of its experience, is the instrument for the transcendent power; and this power is encountered in the dance directly, instantly and without intermediaries. The body is experienced as having a spiritual, inner dimension as a channel for the descent of the power.

Man apprehends and has knowledge of his own being only in as far as he is able to visualize it in the image of his gods, who constitute the measure of his penetration into the mystery of being. The emancipation of man in relation to his god is achieved through imitation of him; and man himself turns creator in doing what the gods do.

In the rhythm of the body and sound are combined all the possibilities of embodying and expressing invisible power, all the strivings and aspirations of the mind, as well as the veiling and protecting of these. Every dance, in imitating the characteristics of the deity adored, is a mimed metamorphosis that seeks to change the dancer into a god or any other worshipped form of existence. This endeavour finds expression in the Hermetic dictum:

> *If you cannot equate yourself with God,*
> *You cannot know him,*
> *For like is known by like.*

Responding and attempting to encompass the phenomenal world outside, man, by dancing, is at the same time put in touch with his own inner being; for, just as creation hides the creator, the physical form of man conceals the spiritual being. The imitation of God works the alchemy of transmuting fear into rapture. In the dance man transcends fragmentation, which is the result of the mirror-trick that split the All into the many; and for the time of the dance he feels again at one with himself and the world around. On this profound level, in the experience of seizure and rapture, there falls to man a universal relatedness, a sense of the totality of life.

This idea is illustrated in the legend of the god Krishna, who, youthful and charming, was once moving among the dwellings of the cowherds. Every maiden who saw him was attracted by his beauty and charm and asked him to dance with her. To each one he promised his appearance for the dance on the night of the full moon, at which time there assembled sixteen hundred maidens. This was the occasion when the miracle of the god was performed: he appeared as a separate Krishna to each maiden, who believed that she alone was dancing with her beloved Lord.

Man and the universe, microcosm and macrocosm, universally follow the same laws. The place where god, the sacred, is manifested becomes the centre of worship; it is an experience within the inner centre of man, as well as a locality without; and man, as the experiencing medium, is the pivot of the encounter with the gods.

The cosmos, like a drink composed of mixed ingredients, needs to be stirred up from time to time so that it does not disintegrate into its constituent elements. Through movement the substance of the creator comes to be dispersed throughout matter; it is in this sense that the cosmos is his dancing ground, his theatre, and that the events in the sky and on earth are the revelation of his power, which carries all in descending and ascending motion.

Creation shows itself, in the annual renewal of nature, and in a series of dissolutions and rebirths, as the 'Great Change': the vast impartially regulated cycle to which man strives to conform. It is a divinely ordered world in which a conflict of powers is immanent; behind lies the Eternally Constant whose nature remains inscrutable. This process or story of the divine is a self-revelation of the god; and yet, because of the limitation and fragmentation inherent in matter, it is also his veiling. The earthly situation, which implies the divine, shows man as the hero of his own drama of life, but also as just another actor in the greater play, an evanescent figure in the eternal round of Life-through-Death, which goes on regardless of who lives or dies. All essential experience is a self-exploration of Life; the measure of man's achievement is his adjustment, without fear, to the universal circumstance of change.

The earliest view of time was cyclic, not linear: an unending succession of birth and death. The new and full moon were the earliest sacred times. Time indicators were the moon's phases, the sun's advance along its pathway of stars, and the cycle of seasonal advance and retreat. The idea of the moon as the ruler over everything which is subject to cyclic change – vegetation, fertility, woman, birth – inspired the belief that death was never permanent, but that everything underwent a process of maturing and decline and that life was always born anew. Lunar orientation appeared as the result of the recognition of analogies between human existence and the processes of plant and animal life. Solar orientation arose from the observation that the sun always remains the same without any becoming, but describes a path, manifest in the succession of day and night and the solstices and equinoxes, following one another in mathematically calculable order. The sun, for man, became the symbol of the succession of life and death, as part of the greater cycle which begins with creation and ends with the *eschaton*, the end of all time. Time, as a vast cycle, was thus a revelation of God's purpose.

To enter sacred time in the dance is to enter the eternal and timeless, which is identical with the here and now. To become one with all creation is the mark of the divine, and for man signifies paradise. This condition implies that the created world, and thus time and motion, are transcended, and the original union, *stasis*, achieved.

Life, from the very first, is bound up with transformation: to be separated, reunited, change form and condition, die and be reborn, act, cease, wait and rest and then act again, is the universal condition of being in the world. For early man, each thing had its own mysterious incalculable aspect; it might at any time challenge him, overwhelm him through its 'appearance'; that is, persecute him with an experience of revelation. Such revelatory knowledge is direct, deeply emotional and inarticulate, the 'I' remaining passive. The experience of awe indicates the tension of the relationship between the power and man: to fear, love and serve the god appear everywhere as related concepts.

Consciousness, when still dormant amid the wealth of intricate relationships, which make up the cosmos, does not reflect about itself; it just responds spontaneously to every stimulus. It is only much later that the power of reason and reflection takes over from ecstatic expression, and knowing action supplants unwitting impulse.

We respond before we question; and every 'appearance' of the power, which man has come to worship as sacred, expresses itself in a deep commotion within the soul of man, which then results in movement: 'When the heart throbs with exhilaration and rapture becomes intense and the agitation of ecstasy is manifested . . . that agitation is neither foot-play nor bodily indulgence, but a dissolution of the soul. . . . It is a state that cannot be explained in words. "Without experience no knowledge"' (Al-Hujwiri).

Through observation, through his imaginative faculty, and through speculative thinking, man sets up structures to protect himself from the chaos of experience, in an endeavour to localize the sacred. Man worshipped nature as long as he felt crushed by her power, and ceased to do so when his technology appeared to have subdued her. To influence the universe, man had first to make it his possession.

At first man worshipped those aspects of nature which appeared to him the most powerful and to which he felt most related: animals, snow-capped mountains, the darkness of caves, woods, trees, stones, rivers. Later all these aspects of power, personified by the multiform divinities, drew together into one god; and then that god became man projected into space. Only very slowly did man withdraw the projections with which he had peopled the empty world—the hierarchies of gods and demons, heavens and hells – and begin to experience the creative fullness of his own psyche. The guide to this inward world was to lie in the many meditative psychotechnic practices that came into existence round the world.

All dance, being imitative, aims at achieving identity with the thing observed and danced out. It is and gives ecstasy by virtue of being in touch with the life-force. The mind is in the twilight state beyond thinking and willing, where something else moves it – just as we, in our best moments, have the feeling of being lived by Life.

Apart from simply being the delight in rhythmic motion, dance is basically a recreation of all kinds of occurrences from life in rhythmic play. Dance-drama arises only much later, when the past begins to be brought intentionally into the dance-theme.

The sacred dance traditions of the world show a truly amazing abundance of imagined forms through which men, everywhere, have sought to relate themselves to the wonder of existence. Its heritage is a reflection of the never-ending play of Life with its own created forms. By acting out his inner experiences, man gains clarity about the nature of the images generated in his own psyche, through which he is able to relate to outward creation. In this way, external actions and inner experience cannot be separated, because the essence of both is wholeness and integration.

The spiritual unity of the human race existed long before any attempt was made to collect and compare the relics of civilizations. Surveying the spiritual traces of times past, we discover in ourselves sympathetic chords that link the old with the new. The modern mentality has turned to the psyche as a last resort, as everything of divine and demonic origin projected out must eventually return to the soul from whence it sprang, to the still-unknown inner self of man. No longer involved with the natural world which has become a thing, his thing, man feels himself to be isolated in the cosmos, a stranger, and has need to find his inner roots.

The sacred traditions of the world are an abundant repository of man's symbols as metaphors of the Mystery. They show his limitations, his idiosyncrasies; yet through them shines universal law. They afford a glimpse of the source, of the encounter with the miraculous, which for man is the ONE experience that validates the drama of creation.

The human psyche, as the source of all religious and cultural phenomena, stores the knowledge man had accumulated before the advent of self-awareness. To establish the link with this buried treasure through the aid of his conscious mind, to realize the images dormant in his psyche, has become a cultural necessity if man is to regain wholeness.

With the dawn of consciousness the world became ambivalent, sundered into opposites by cognition, which opened up a deep chasm between spontaneity and reflection. Ego-consciousness brought with it a sense of loneliness, its genesis being experienced as guilt and suffering, as inevitable punishment. Today man suffers from the illusion that the entire universe is held together by the categories of human thought, fearing that if he does not cling to them with the utmost tenacity, everything will vanish into chaos. Yet, at the point where we experience reality most intimately, we understand it least.

Ritual and the gods

Praise ye the Lord. Praise God in his sanctuary: praise him in the firmament of his power.
Praise him for his mighty acts: praise him according to his excellent greatness.
Praise him with the sound of the trumpet: praise him with the psaltery and harp.
Praise him with the timbrel and dance: praise him with stringed instruments and organs.
Praise him upon the loud cymbals: praise him upon the high sounding cymbals.
Let every thing that hath breath praise the Lord. Praise ye the Lord.

(Psalm 150.)

In spite of all his knowledge about himself, man remains his own greatest mystery and adventure. Ultimately, he cannot identify with any one thing, all outer phenomena presenting him with only a partial aspect of himself. Conditioned by the I-Thou relationship, he is placed between the inner world of the psyche and the outer world of 'sense objects', forever in transition between the two, having to balance inner perception and experience with adaptation to outward circumstance. The eclipse of the god as the unifying factor for all experience, and his remoteness and silence, lead man to invoke and search for him.

In dance ritual – and all early ritual is dance – man undertook to represent his god, celebrating and commemorating the god's measured movements in creation and the traces of his journey on earth. Man sets out to make present the divine actions at the beginning of time and, through precise repetition of the rite throughout millennia, to anticipate time's end. By dancing out again and again the original Mystery of Creation, the dancer, as the interpreting medium and centre of the rite, is put in touch with the primal event, which, at the same time, transforms the dance into an act of self-realization, both aspects being necessary ingredients for the promotion of life, on the cosmic as well as on the individual plane.

All mythologies contain the idea of the gradual running-down of the universe, and of the cataclysm at the end of time; nature requires renewal, and the perennial function of ritual is to release life, to compensate for the work of time. Thus the historical situation is brought in touch with timeless, primordial reality, the essential truth of which is periodically manifested through the enactment of ritual. Thus emotional tensions are released, and new hope is engendered, in respect of human needs ranging from the crises in man's individual life, and their seasonal counterparts in nature and the cosmos, to the assurance of the eternal bliss which will be achieved through the final transformation. For ritual to fulfil its proper function, therefore, it must always be a symbolic representation of Ultimate Reality. The danced rite is thus a metaphysical necessity, combining human circumstance and cosmic events, even though the profound seriousness of the ideal life might be masked by mimicry and play.

As a symbolic representation of a primordial event, the dance is performed with careful attention to detail, so as to ensure the efficacy of the rite, which sets out to invoke the transcendent power and utilize its influence. Typical sounds and movements, pertaining to tribes and races, are so deeply rooted that they persist for thousands of years without substantial changes. Through exact repetition of sacred dance movements, experiences are evoked which relate to their origin, the participant voluntarily entering the play-world of the gods with the aim of becoming like them. Ritual dancing is never aimed at an audience, but rather involves all those present; the rite itself is addressed exclusively to the divinity.

Man has a deep-seated urge to mask the mystery of the transformation of the divine into matter and of man into god; but there is also that in man which wants to put on show what is most sacred to him, dress it up and present it as a spectacle to an audience. But as soon as a rite thus becomes a mere spectacle, seeking to influence man rather than commune with God, its universal power is broken and it disintegrates. Religion separates itself from dance, and art from work; the sacred becomes profane entertainment; and old rituals, relegated to the margins of a new life, degenerate into social habits and become folk-dances and games.

As a symbolic expression of man's understanding of the world, dance ritual reveals a reality which transcends empirical reasoning and abstract cosmological speculation. At most times, for most peoples, it has been the central concern of their lives; from it have later emerged all the arts. Some instant or fragment of life, it was felt, some potency had to be arrested, the experience of it repeated and celebrated so as to have an established relationship to it, thereby solidifying the flux of life and giving it support. Ritual strengthens the growth of consciousness by providing it with a frame of reference. Dance ritual throughout the ages is a self-delineation of developing man; it promotes by analogy the leap beyond the confines of consciousness, and it bridges the chasm between spontaneity and reflection.

The order of life was seen to be sacred; in it the divine pattern expressed itself. In antiquity, almost all human activities were sacraments, and only in modern times has there been a progressive secularization of human actions and hence an increasing bondage to time. In the divinely ordered cosmos, older gods recede and younger ones rise to take their place in the consciousness of man, the god beheld being a function of the consciousness of the beholder.

Man may worship the gods with the same intensity everywhere, but they do not always reveal themselves equally. The gods of the oldest times are animals, and only much later do they appear in human form, accompanied by holy animals or other attributes. Before men can raise themselves above the animal, they must first be able to perceive the divine in human form.

As soon as man knows the god's name, i.e. his special function and power, he begins to be able to do something about him. In this way mythology is born. Every experience of power thus leads to it being given a form, and every god who is established as such represents so much consciousness gained. Even for modern man, in all cases where conscious manipulation fails – as it does at times of crisis, such as birth, love, conflict, death – the 'gods' continue to wield their influence. The actual images of any structuring system are derived from a given locality; and yet their functions are universal.

To be inspired by tradition is to render the individual fit for the community. Until recent times, no man could, with impunity, step outside a tradition. In order to understand and be attuned to the world, he needed only to know the myths, take part in ritual and decipher its symbols; through them he was linked to both the inner and outer worlds. The heroic man was not the one who tried to reform the existing order, but he who had the courage to affirm it, and who did so repeatedly on every occasion of his encounter with the sacred.

Since the gods occupy only their respective limited territories, they have need of messengers, through whom they extend their dominion into every sphere. As a result of the plasticity of their ethereal body, divine beings may assume any shape or dissolve their bodies at will. Such was the insight of man in early history, who saw all physical processes as caused by powerful spiritual beings. In constant movement, these beings linked the above with the below, both descending into manifestation and elevating what is manifest to its spiritual source. Their presence was felt particularly strongly at the crucial times of life and death and during the ecstasy of the dance.

The divine immaterial substance, when it manifests itself in the innermost or lower-most regions of creation, is cloaked in the material substance of all spheres through which it has travelled, thereby acquiring ever greater density. The struggle between the light and dark aspects, as the manifest dual symptoms of the single unity which is life, takes place on all levels of creation, imparting to life its dramatic quality.

Life, death, rebirth

Sleep and death are the decisive experiences which reveal the division between body and spirit. In the encounter with death is to be found the root of every form of worship. The mystery of death constitutes the greatest challenge for the human mind, and the earliest cults known are cults of the dead.

The celebration of funerary ritual is based on the belief that death is only another aspect of life, and that it is the duty of the living to assist the deceased in his resurrection. The dancing of such ritual portrays, on the whole, the battle of the deceased with the demons of darkness and his final victory over them. The dancing is given emphasis by strong rhythms, loud musical accompaniment and the wailing of the mourners. In Egypt, funerary ritual achieved gigantic proportions. It was carried out to an elaborate pattern; in the case of the burial of a pharaoh, this involved the whole community in magic support. Encircling dances at the bier or funeral pyre were universal, as an invocation of the power of life and as a protection against the power of darkness.

The light and dark aspects of life together make up its balanced totality, and have indeed been honoured equally. Death reveals the deeper mystery of life, by causing change and transformation. It is only when the god appropriates to himself the light or good aspects exclusively, the dark, evil aspects being transferred to the wholly other (as in the Christian idea of the Devil) that the dance, as an experience of *total* possession by the power, begins to be forbidden and disappears from worship in favour of quietist meditative practices and the spoken word. Demonic beings, as personifications of the irrational, dark aspects of experience, always precede the god of monotheistic religions, and are seen as evil only when brought into contact with the latter.

In most cultures, however, the 'sub-human' or demonic, and the angelic or 'super-human', were felt to belong equally to the realm of the divine. Terrible demons in the iconography of the world's sacred traditions always wear masks, and are often por-trayed as dancing in blazing flames, fire or heat being a symbol of transformation. In this form the power impersonates the dark aspect of creation, the devouring, terrible side of necessity, without which no development is possible. In the ecstasy of the dance, when fear is magically transformed into rapture, there is revealed behind the terrifying mask of the demon a beneficent guide. To embrace the duality of nature, to give oneself to the dance, is to guard against separation; life in its totality goes on, in its eternal alternation of foul and fair, until its tasks have been accomplished.

In its earliest forms the rite was always walked or danced in the form of a labyrinth or spiral. Both are images of the wanderings of the spirit, of entering by way of a gate into the maze of darkness, or death, and of then going back, attaining rebirth. Death, as the master of all that is under the sun, was experienced and portrayed as the final achievement of life, as its ultimate task and necessary preliminary to a new birth. Rebirth, therefore, was the central aim of the cult of the dead, demonstrating the continuity of life in the sense of a constant renewal of the eternal divine potency, and showing the deep link between death and conception.

In all forms of worship it was essential to ensure a permanent link with the primal deity, in whatever form it happened to be worshipped. Death, gestation and birth were for this reason also repeated ritually, symbolically, as an attempt to foster the renewal and rebirth of the 'soul' of the primal deity, and as an expression of man's desire to manipulate the life-sustaining power for his own purposes. In this way the dance is a response to both the call of life and that of death, affirming the Mysterious as a dimension of existence.

The spirit as ancestor

The law . . . and the ordinance which I have taught and preached unto you,
These are your master when I am gone hence.

(*Bhagavad Gita.*)

In terms of life on earth, movement is the conquest of death, and the 'appearance' of the Divine was therefore worshipped in movement. In the dance there occurs an identification with the manifest aspects of the divinity through outward imitation, as well as an inward assimilation of its qualities. Occasions for dancing and magic rites were all major events and seasons: birth, puberty, wedding, battle, victory, death, the hunt, seed time and harvest, as well as any sudden, inexplicable and frightening event which broke upon the community.

Early man lived in constant terror which justified perpetual magic rites to keep the fearful aspects of life at bay. Every unexpected event roused suspicion and fear, and each new activity bore the mark of the dread of becoming. For this reason every important phase was initiated with a magic rite to avert evil and encourage the good. Sacred ceremonies raise the group to an intensity of shared emotion, whereby the power is created by which it may communicate with the divinity.

Dancing has always been a community activity, uniting sound, rhythm and movement. It expresses itself in the urge to release psychological tensions, in the play of limbs which leads to rhythmically regulated movements, clapping of hands, slapping of thighs, stamping of feet; in the early stages of the dance the human body itself was the sound-producing instrument.

On the whole, the sexes were segregated during dancing. Men's dances far exceeded women's dances in number. Men alone executed sun, war and nearly all animal-spirit dances, as well as rain and shamanistic medicine dances; in fact, women were only rarely permitted to join in tribal animal and mask dances. On the other hand, in the planter cultures, women were often the only participants in the fertility dances, in certain rain and harvest dances, during birth rituals, at the consecration of girls, at moon worship and during mourning ritual. Circular and choral dances, as being the oldest, were only gradually superseded by line-dances where the participants face one another, as especially in war dances where the chorus divides itself into two hostile groups. Couple-dances belong chiefly to mating and wedding ceremonies, but also occur in battle rituals as imitative of single combat.

Animal dances are accompanied by nature sounds and by those appropriate to the animal, introverted mystical dances by low, aspirated humming sounds, and the ecstasy of wild leaping or whirling dances by powerful shouts and cries. The original time-beater is the stamping foot to which is added a sharper sound by the clapping of hands or by slapping some part of the body. The matriarchal early planters invented the drum, which underlines the dancing with a regular *ostinato* sound; the slit drum, a hollowed cut trunk split lengthwise, is a symbol of the feminine, the flute a symbol of the phallus and fertility. The basic sound patterns were enriched by the use of stamping-poles, and by attaching rattling ornaments to the body. The use of melodic instrumental music to accompany the dance is a late development which grew out of the early dance-song, musical accompaniment being at first always sung by the dancer himself, thereby creating a spiritual connection between the theme and magic purpose of the dance. In religious dance rites the music tends to be intoned in a liturgical manner, syllabic psalmody heightening the ecstatic quality of any ritual of union. The unrestrained outcry, from which the voice abruptly falls without any gradation between tension and release, as well as the excited, emphatic utterance, are expressions of ecstasy.

Man was taught to dance by the animals, which he observed closely and learned to imitate. He depended on them for his food, clothing, tools and weapons, and therefore needed to study their habits and characteristics. Man, the hunter, was totally identified with the ways of his prey; and the totem-animal which embodied the spirit of the tribe's ancestor was not only the source of his livelihood, but also his god. The ancestor was the bearer of all the forces of nature; as such he was the spirit of fertility, victory, death and birth. In the animal as ancestor, man admired all those qualities which he himself lacked. He admired the bear's strength as being greater than his own, or the swiftness of birds and their capacity for flight. The more completely the dancer achieved identification with the god, the greater the magic potency of the ritual.

In ancient Mexico a festival took place every eight years, at a time when the vegetation was resting; this was the festival of the dance of the gods. The dancers wore animal skins and feathers and covered their heads with masks. In such dances the leader of the tribe or community, as the ancestor's representative on earth, endeavoured to imitate the shape and movements of the animal as precisely as he could, as this was believed to be the sure way of assimilating the animal's physical and spiritual qualities. The animal imitated was to be affected by man's sympathetic response to it, so that it would comply with his expectations and demands.

The Wadda tribe of Ceylon had a traditional hunting dance, in which one of the dancers shot at a tuft of grass representing a wild boar. Having wounded the animal, he continued his dance, pretending to follow the wounded boar. Suddenly he sank on to one knee and dragged the other leg after him, which signified that the boar in his turn had attacked and wounded the dancer. After careful treatment of the leg the animal was eventually killed by the hunter. Man wished either to placate and subdue the animal's powers or to gain them for himself. The wild beast may have been hostile to early man, but it was never unrelated, since it was connected with the hunter by mysterious spiritual bonds.

In many regions, especially in the tropics, certain animals were thought to influence the weather, and especially to have the power to bring rain at times of drought; to imitate the movements of these animals was to induce rain to fall. This, for instance, was the nature of the Australian Aborigines' kangaroo dance. When the kangaroo had become rare during times of drought, so that the tribe was beginning to have difficulty in tracking it down, its members imitated the animal's leaps and jumps: 'When the dancers had put on a tail they began to move about like a group of kangaroos. They would take a leap forward and then sit down and scratch themselves, as is the habit of kangaroos when warming themselves in the sun. One man would beat the rhythm of the dance with a club on a shield, while two others carried weapons and slowly followed the animal dancers everywhere, stealthily creeping up to them, so that then they could stab them with their lances' (R. Sonner, *Musik und Tanz*).

By this act of imitative magic the balance of nature was to be restored and rain would surely come; harmonious integration with the forces of nature was the greatest boon that tribal religion could bestow.

Every dance divides the members of the community into active and passive: the person identified with the animal spirit, demon or god – the shaman – and the others who witness the transformation and revelation. For the shaman, the dance is part of his function of linking the tribe with the ancestral spirit; it serves as a channel for divine power in all his tasks, including those of healing and exorcism. In the exorcistic dances the shaman chants, beats his drum and makes wild, ecstatic movements which represent his pursuit of evil spirits. In his dance he fights with them, and with changed voice, that is with the voice of the ancestral spirit, persuades them to leave the sick man, whom he encircles and to whom he transmits the healing powers. Through his ecstatic dance-journey to the beyond he achieves communion with the supernatural. The meeting with the other world is the result of an expansion of consciousness; the shaman is taken over by the spirit which speaks and acts through him.

Thus, the change in consciousness is seen as the advent of the god, who finally takes possession of man, using the worshipper as his vessel, the instrument for making known his will. The worshipper, on the other hand, utilizes the divine power in himself for the purpose of acting in the world in honour of his god, working miracles, giving oracles, building sanctuaries, bearing witness.

Since possession and seizure cause strong forces to take over in man and let him experience a measure of freedom from the limitations of his body and the state of ordinary perception, they are methodically sought after in cult and ritual; the contact with transcendental forces guarantees a life of heightened quality. The structure of all ritual is built on the principle of the gradual intensification of experience, the climax being catharsis.

The cult of the goddess Cybele, one of the many personifications of the Great Mother, spread from Asia Minor to Greece and Italy. It was celebrated by her priests, the Corybantes, to the accompaniment of the wild noise of drums, cymbals, pipes and rattles, while the dancers whirled about in ecstatic trance, hair flying, uttering piercing cries and shouts. The climax of the rite was often the self-castration of the priests as the sign of their total surrender to the goddess. Similarly, the cult of the god Dionysus, or Bacchus, contained orgiastic rites, which led the initiate to abandon himself totally to his instinctual nature and thereby experience in full the creative power of the god. The initiating agent was wine, and one of the many symbols of the cult was the thyrsos-staff, surmounted by a phallic cone. The ecstatic dances of the Maenads at the time of spring gave expression to the blinding sensuous epiphany of the god. According to the testimony of Diodorus: 'In many towns of Greece, every alternate year, Bacchanalian assemblies of women gather together, and it is the custom for maidens to carry the thyrsos and to revel together, honouring and glorifying the god; and for the married women to worship the god in organized bands and to revel in every way to celebrate the presence of Dionysus, imitating the Maenads, who of old, it is said, constantly attended the god.'

To agricultural peoples, the times of sowing and harvesting were the most vital, and were therefore sacred; they were celebrated by sacrificial offerings to the gods of earth and sky. To leap around the seedlings was an effort to force the seed to grow. The higher the jump, the higher the plant was likely to be. Stamping dances were equally common, as a way to ensure the fertility of the earth, rhythmic stamping being analogous to the creative rhythm of the phallus. Fertility dances, being always accompanied by strong rhythms, were often representations of the sexual act or ended in mass copulation. The sprouting of the seed was associated with the fertilized womb, and the fertilizing power in nature was worshipped as the manifestation of the god, the bringing forth of fruit through the life-creating power of the Earth Mother.

The dance, as the corporeal image of growth and disintegration, is the most ancient form of magic. Mythologically, the coming of light, the beginning of the world, denotes the discovery of subjective reality, the ability of man to reflect, stand apart and look on evolution, the capacity to perceive his actions in relation to the sacred, the awareness that he is circumscribing the unknown from many sides. The magical forms whereby man comes to terms with life are anthropocentric systems of world domination. At all times it is man who is the measure of all things, of the world he creates and reflects, and of how he responds to it. Some symbols carry the 'world-feeling' of so great a number of people, and exercise such compulsion, that they impart a sense that life itself depends on their preservation and re-enactment: the hunter is identified with the totem-animal, the planter with the earth, seed and crop and the conditions of the atmosphere, that is with his gods; the gods of religion ultimately become principles, functions of consciousness, and modern man is identified with mere abstractions, the 'isms' on which he believes his life depends.

When man turned to the sky and tried to penetrate into the order of the stellar world, he identified the movement of his gods with those of the sun, moon and other planets. There are innumerable sun-worship dance rituals in the sacred traditions of the world. At midsummer the Mandan Indians celebrated their great sun dance, which was preceded by a number of secret preparatory rites. The sun-pole was erected in the centre of a large enclosed area; nearby stood the altar, adorned with the symbols of the tribe. The dancers were painted and, encircling the pole, fixed their gaze on the sun symbol at its top. Similarly, the Navajo celebrated the rebirth of the sun in winter, at night, in an enclosed area, which could only be entered from its east side. In the centre of the sacred precinct a pile of wood was set on fire, whereupon the young men of the tribe, painted white, danced round the fire in the direction of the sun's path, the rising of which they portrayed symbolically; singing and dancing, they hoisted an image of the sun on the central pole. For a while it hovered at the top and was then let down again. This dance was followed by a fertility ritual, during which a seed was planted; during the dance this was made to grow symbolically, and at the end of the dance it bore fruit. With sunrise the dance came to an end, having found its climax in a wild, whirling movement. Now the sacred area was open on all four sides.

Celestial motion being circular, man, by imitating it, partakes of the cosmic dance-round and begins to experience reality as order round a centre: the ancestral god is he who is immovably centred. This experience of the centre becomes basic to worship and eventually results in man's orientation toward an objective reality.

Plotinus in his *Enneads* comments on this experience of the centre, using an image borrowed from the antique chorus which moved, singing and dancing, round its leader or round the altar: 'Just as the chorus always moves in a circle around the leader, and sings best when it turns towards him, so we must also surround him, and when we regard him we can behold our end and our place, our voice is in harmonious accord with him and we dance around him in a dance inspired by truth. In this dance we can find the source of life, the source of intelligence, the principle of existence, the cause of goodness and the origin of the soul.'

The more undifferentiated the psychic phenomena in man, the more he is identified with bodily events. All religious experience was originally entirely physical, the senses playing a decisive part. From this all-absorbing experience of the body arose the notion that the deity physically enters man, who is thus transfigured. Equally, union with the god was gained directly by eating part of him, thereby acquiring spiritual qualities by a transmutation of substance within the worshipper. This religious rite is, for example, preserved in the celebration of the Eucharist: the god's creative death is a sacrifice, the offering up of life.

The body's own potency turns the dance into a sacrament. In early history the body as a whole, as well as each separate aspect, was sacred. Food, drink, breath and copulation were regarded as sacred channels for the power to enter man; and the body's sacred power was expressed in the symbolic ornamentation of the whole body or part of it. Body-painting signifies dynamic transformation; and as the ornamented vessel, as the dwelling-place of the power, as the city of God, the body is sacred. The head was often covered or masked as being the seat of the power, just as in ritual sacrifice the surrender of the head denoted total sacrifice. To put on another face with the help of the mask was to admit another spirit; by the loss of one's own shape and physiognomy the transformation into the god had become evident.

Masked dances were a deliberate means of approaching the nature of the sacred animal, and thereby approaching the god who dwelt in the same disguise. Head-dress, skins and posture were outward aids to an inward assimilation. The features given special emphasis were the eyes, marking the 'appearance' of the power, and the mouth, as the symbol of the twofold aspect of the divine, both bringing forth and devouring.

Ritual transformation, the cathartic climax of all sacred dances, rested on the insight that physical birth produces only the physical man, and that the living spirit has to be brought into being by a second birth. All transformations, being vested with profound mystery, need the protective mask to facilitate the process. Transformation of matter, through the heat generated in the ecstasy of the dance, becomes most evident in the alchemy which transforms the human personality. All growth and development presupposes transformation, which on a psychological level is equivalent to dying to one's previous existence: the god is revealed behind the mask of the animal. The ecstatic experience which gives birth to the Mystery is that of passing beyond the 'death' of the body to become transfigured like the god.

Sacred space

Despite the apparent tumult on the surface, everything is harmony at root. Shiva's dance, taking place both at the centre of the universe and in the heart of man, symbolizes the union of time and space within evolution, the incarnation of timeless energy, which manifests in the dual aspects of nature. He dances to maintain the life of the cosmos and to give release to those who seek him.

Transformation, as the purpose of all ritual practices, is synonymous with the revelation of man's innermost being by touching the centre, the unifying practice of the dance counteracting differentiation and the creation of ever more complicated relationships throughout the millions of years of development.

The continuous coming face-to-face with the divine centre was celebrated in the ritual encircling of sacred sites, objects or persons, as well as in round dances around a holy centre. To circumscribe the centre was to be in constant relationship with the source of being. Thereby geography was transformed into symbolic cosmology, and man at its centre became the cosmocrator.

Space provided man with one of his deepest experiences; and, as the body was felt to possess magical reference, so did space outside. Its three dimensions, each having two possible directions of movement implying two poles, became zones where the sacred was experienced and worshipped. The beginning of both time and creation pertains to the centre. From this focal point manifestations radiate out in concentric rings. This universal experience has found expression in the many circumambulation rites and round dances of the sacred traditions of the world.

From the centre the vertical and horizontal axes reach out, establishing the dimensions of time and space. Concentrically arranged, everything is linked in constant relationship. The circle's four points, where the two axes meet it, are seen to be the four turning-points in the sun's path, the circle itself symbolizing the creation of light in space.

The vertical and horizontal axes are, in many cultures, associated with the image of the Tree of Life, the vertical axis being the road of descent and ascent of the power and the horizontal axis its manifestation in creation. In the Axis Mundi or centre of the world, all pairs of opposites come together.

In this static cross, the place of the interaction of macrocosm and microcosm, stands man.

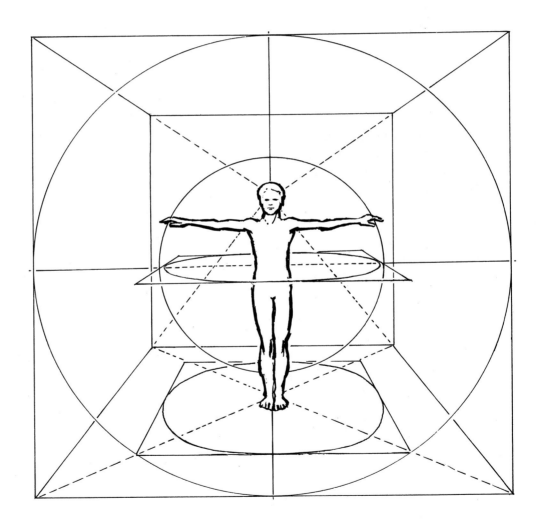

Human anatomy, with its six-pointed orientation in space, has as its invisible seventh point, where the axes intersect in the centre of man, the 'cave of the heart', which is the battleground of the dual forces of life. The subdivision of this static cross produces the dynamic cross or moving wheel, symbol of man's potential for orientation and movement in space, cyclic motion being made possible through the interplay of opposites.

Sacred structured space facilitates orientation, provides the framework for worship, and transforms chaos into cosmos, thus making human life possible. The form of the temple, as the external place of worship was first assimilated from the earth □, symbol of space, and the sky ⌒, symbol of time: ⊟. This spatial concept was equally applied to the human body which, as the sacred vessel, is the actual place of the ritual transformation. Spiritual and physiological transformations are identified with terrestrial transitions; i.e. they are expressed in spatial relationships.

Preparation for the sacred dance is often marked by a period of prayer, when the worshipper either lies on the ground in prostration before his god or kneels in a foetal position, invoking the power; the divine is as yet unmanifest, has not been born in him. Only with the entry of the 'spirit' into man does he become fully human; and he is then called upon to relate himself to the time-space dimension in action. By virtue of being centred, thereby having both a focus and a direction, man's actions become sacred.

There are very many possible combinations of foot, arm, head and body positions within these spatial coordinates, as the structured manifestation of the spiritual dimension of the sacred around the worshipper. In adoration and praise, as one newly born, man raises his arms; to lower them shows the position in which the Tree of Life lowers its branches at death. Reaching out horizontally, man establishes communication. The same closed or open positions may be taken up by the legs and feet. The rear and left sides are identified with the past, with involution, the unconscious zone or origin; the front and right with the future, evolution and consciousness, being the zone of outcome. The Hindu and Buddhist traditions distinguish seven centres or wheels of energy in the human body, the chakras, stretching along the spine from the perineum to the crown of the head. The 'frontal eye', the square inch between the eyes, as the dwelling place of the primal spirit, is not represented as a bodily organ, but contains all reality; it represents the Present which is timeless and without extension.

To pass through the projected sacred diagrams during the rituals in the sacred precinct is to be brought back to wholeness, for which orientation along the structured mandala is a guide. Sacred space offers a centre for communication with the power. It is the locality where its dramatic breakthrough into the world is commemorated.

Sacred space, as the structured locality where man has established the dominion of his gods, is the known space, the locality where the power manifests and repeats its revelation; it is the place where the god has stopped in movement and has created. This site, by virtue of man's acts of worship, becomes a centre for communion. Outside this enclosed area, beyond the known world, is the realm of chaos, the terrifying unknown space where forms disintegrate.

All sacred constructions represent the universe in symbolic form. The closing of the sacred precinct with gates was essential if the rite was to be effective, safeguarding and concentrating the influence issuing from the sacred object, animal or person within the confined area. To it lead sacred paths along which pilgrimages were, and still are, made for renewed contact with the power. Circumambulation of sacred mountains, trees, temples and shrines is one of the oldest of religious activities and has been practised universally since megalithic times.

The sanctuary's holy of holies is often wholly or partly below ground (cave, Mithraeum, crypt), as being the central part of the sacred edifice and therefore not visible or directly accessible to the worshipper. He walks or dances round the sanctuary, whereby he is radially connected with the centre (Mount Kailas, Ka'aba, Borobudur stupa). He may also ascend to the sanctuary, if it is built on high ground (or if it is itself a holy mountain, representing the world-navel). The inner, temporal axis is often crowned by a pinnacle, spire or holy figure. The 'Way of the Cross' is still walked in procession, marked by its stations, often winding up a hill in ascending sequence outside the church, or laid out in an open space nearby; alternatively, the sacred path is commemorated by the priest and congregation making a circuit of the church and ending at the altar.

The stupa of Borobudur, as a Buddhist symbol of the cosmos, represents along the vertical axis the ascent in four layers from the world of desire and illusion via the world of forms and the formless to Absolute Beatitude, represented by the symbol of the Buddha as Vajrasattva, turning the Wheel of the Law. He is seated at the centre, at the hub of the wheel on which the contraries turn.

This stupa was circumambulated and ascended by the worshipper. During such ritual processions prayers were chanted, mantras repeated, prayer wheels turned, and the air was purified with incense to heighten the efficacy of the rite. The devotees move in ecstatic joy round the living presence residing at the centre; through the outward act of encircling a reorientation takes place towards the Within. The act of encircling is a symbolic expression of the aspirations of man, which for ever revolve about his knowledge of the creative centre.

The deity, the sacred centre, also needs the worshipper. Ibn Arabi, for example, taught that the Ka'aba is animated by those who walk around it. Analogous to the external act of encircling is the *tawaf*, the encircling of the heart, as man's inner Ka'aba which during worship is recharged with life. Man's second birth, his 'completion', is effected by a historically determined tradition, which thus renders it a vital tool for initiation into a community's mysteries and a vessel for the Spirit; 'It is sown a natural body, it is raised a spiritual body.'

Cross-section and plan
of Borobudur stupa, Java

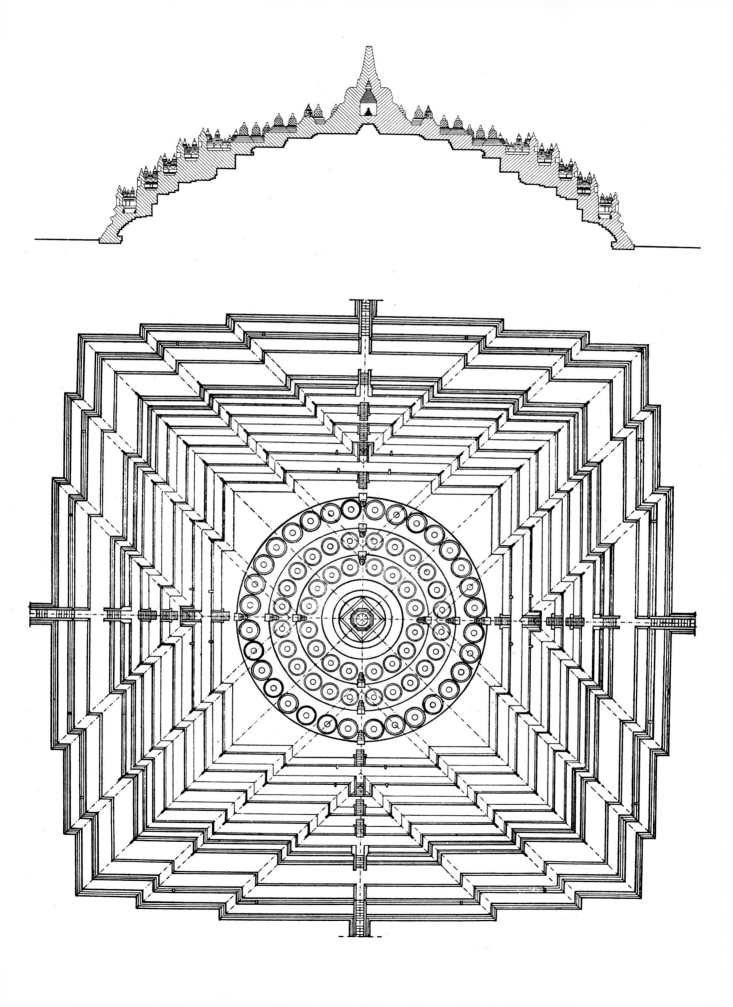

'And just as he who dances with his body, rushing through the rotating movements of the limbs, acquires a right to share in the round dance, in the same way, he who dances the spiritual dance, always moving in the ecstasy of faith, acquires a right to dance in the ring of all creation' (St Ambrose, Bishop of Milan, fourth century).

Through the dance, man attains the state that renders his work into service; this presupposes the dancer's 'death' and 'resurrection' by way of sacrifice, which is the pattern of the great cycle of being-in-life-through-mutual-killing. The theme of death as the life of the living runs like a red thread through the history of the world's sacred traditions. It is epitomized by the dance of the Hindu mother-goddess Kali, the embodiment of the universe which sends forth beings only to consume them. Death and life appear as transformations of a single indestructible force; life forever offers itself to Life. All forms are the disguises of the Eternal Unchanging.

Sacrifice is central to religion, as the expression of total surrender to the divine. It is synonymous with the bestowal of gifts to promote union, the original union with the deity being restored when the sacrifice is repeated. Human sacrifice was replaced with the sacrificial offering of animals, harvest produce or foodstuffs, as the offering of part of man's acquisitions for the greater glory of his god. Ultimately, it is always the god himself, of whom all these things are aspects, who is being sacrificed.

The spiral, as the schematic image of the evolution of the universe, symbolizes the movement traced by the spirit, and shows the relationship of the circle and its centre. All labyrinth or maze dances mime the journey of the dead, the winding path representing the soul's wanderings: the primal maze at the entrance to the divine world, as traced outside prehistoric cave-sanctuaries, became the mandalic road of high religions.

In the mystic Maro dance of the island of West Ceram, lasting nine nights, the nine families of man are said to have participated. The women sat in the centre, and the men around them danced a large nine-fold spiral. According to myth the maiden Hainu-wele, who during the nine nights had presented man with various implements and skills, was then killed, but her dead and buried body became the source of man's food. In another labyrinth rite, the Malekulan Na-leng, the dancers represented the structure of the labyrinth and provided a running commentary to the dramatization of the journey of the dead. The dance itself was a tribal initiation ceremony in which the neophyte, singing on his way, sought to join the personages in the sanctuary by treading along the path of the labyrinth. The climax of the dance was the ritual marriage, the union within the centre.

The ritual initiations in the Graeco-Oriental mystery cults, as described by Plutarch (*On Isis and Osiris*), equally celebrated spiritual union after a journey along the dark passages of the labyrinth, here in an already somewhat allegorized version: 'Death and initiation clearly correspond, word for word, thing for thing. At first there are wanderings and laborious circuits, and journeyings through the dark, full of misgivings, where there is no consummation; then, before the very end, come terrors of every kind, shivers and trembling, and sweat and amazement. After this a wonderful light meets the wanderer: he is admitted into pure meadow lands where are voices and dances, and the majesty of holy sounds and sacred visions. Here the new initiate, all rites completed, is at large.'

The treading of an obstructed path is the key motif of labyrinth symbolism, the maze being a symbol of the outer shell around the hidden centre. Overcoming the obstacle that obstructs the entry into the centre is equivalent to sacrifice; reaching the place of union in the centre denotes transformation; and re-emergence from it is rebirth.

The Geranos dance of Delos, which commemorates Theseus' wanderings in the Cretan labyrinth, is the historical prototype which influenced the early Christian church dances. The dancers all held a rope, symbolizing Ariadne's thread. As the latter was first unravelled by Theseus and then again rolled into a ball, the dance-leader first led the dancers with it into the centre of the labyrinth and then out again. The dancers, having danced into the labyrinth from right to left, the direction of involution and death, turn round in the centre and, following their leader dance out again, now in the opposite direction, that of evolution and birth. The pattern of the spirals in the Geranos dance signifies the continuation of life beyond death, the intimation of immortality at the very core of human experience.

In early Christian art the Minotaur of the labyrinth came to be identified with Satan, and Theseus became Christ, who descends into the underworld, overcomes Satan and emerges victorious through the gates of the Kingdom of the Dead together with the saved. From the eleventh century onwards labyrinths are to be found in many of the cathedrals and churches of Europe, inlaid in the floor of the nave near the west door. They were conceived of as three-dimensional, with the centre/top being the Heavenly Jerusalem. From early Christian times the sun was a symbol for Christ (*sol invictus, sol justitiae*) as the Sun of Righteousness, risen for all who dwell in darkness, a belief which is connected with the early medieval mystics' idea of the resurrected Christ dancing forth from the underworld.

On the labyrinth in the cathedral of Auxerre, the Pelota ball-game or dance was performed annually on Easter Day, in three-step rhythm (*tripudium*), to the accompaniment of the rhythmic chant of the Easter antiphon. It was danced in a long chain along the labyrinth pattern by the dean (or another senior Church dignitary) and the canons. The ball (*pilota*), which the dean or his deputy had received from the newly inducted canons, was handed down during the dance alternately, in wreathwise fashion along the line of dancers, who also revolved around his own axis. The essence of the dance was the circulation of the ball from the leader of the group to the other members and back from them to the leader, who was probably in the middle of the ring, robed in all his distinctive vestments. When the singing and dancing was over, the dean and chapter joined together in a sacred meal. The probable symbolism of the Pelota dance is the representation of the apparent path or dance of the sun throughout the year, its 'Passion', and the corresponding Passion of creation, analogous to the path of the incarnate Christ, his death, burial and resurrection as the Christ-Sun at Easter.

The earliest known Christian mystery-ritual is the Dance of Jesus, described in the Apocryphal Acts of St John; as late as the fourth century it was still regarded as a ritual of initiation. This danced hymn of praise is a spiritual sacrifice, and at the same time the fulfilment of the Lord's Supper. The inward sacrifice consists in the rendering of praise. Christ stands in the middle, and the twelve apostles walk around him in a circle:

> *He gathered all of us together and said:*
> *Before I am delivered up to them,*
> *let us sing an hymn to the Father,*
> *and so go forth to that which lieth before us.*
> *He bade us therefore make as it were a ring,*
> *holding one another's hands,*
> *and himself standing in the midst he said:*
> *Answer Amen unto me.*
> *He began then to sing an hymn and to say:*
> *Glory be to thee, Father.*
> *And we, going about in a ring, answered him: Amen.*

Through the act of thanksgiving, the rendering of praise and the disciples' identification with their Master, the 'Dance of Jesus' redeems the spirit from the earthly body. The disciple must repeat the acts of his Lord, if he is to become like him, to achieve union with him. Only he who understands the meaning of his acts can understand his essence. This secret is apprehended in the movements of the dance, in the ecstasy it releases. The celebration of the *unio mystica*, wherein the new-born disciple is united with the Master in the mystery of spiritual at-one-ment, is performed after the manner of the ancient mystery cults, here presented with a Christian coating. Such rituals were widespread throughout antiquity, and continued to reappear among Christian communities outside the official Church.

Within the mystic circle the holy office proceeds. The Redeemer descends and rises again, having gathered God's seeds from the world of matter, the disciples, like their Master, being on a voyage bound for heaven. After his transfiguration ('And he stood in the midst of the cave and illumined it') the god no longer has an outward form; the mystery Christ now dwells in the bodies of those that belong to him. All that remains is a voice; and this voice imparts to his disciples symbols by which they may be guided:

> *A torch am I to thee that beholdest me. Amen.*
> *A mirror am I to thee that perceivest me. Amen.*
> *A door am I to thee that knockest at me. Amen.*
> *A way am I to thee a wayfarer. Amen.*

This voice, as the original Sound at the beginning and end of Creation, imparts the essence of its mystery through the dance.

After dancing out the Passion, during which the disciple is profoundly shaken out of his fixed state, and beholds the universal drama of dismemberment and death in life as the epiphany of the divine, he sees the 'Cross of Light' through which the true essence of the Master is revealed. The sacred dance is followed by the *agape*, the love-feast, and the custom of the kiss of peace.

The dance of David before the ark of the covenant became the Old Testament source for sanctioning the dance in the Christian Church: 'Dance the dance of David before the ark of the covenant, for I believe that such a dance holds the mystery of walking in the sight of God' (Gregory of Nazianz, *Theological Orations*).

In the early Christian Church sacred dancing took place in the choir above, with the bishop in the role of leader. The idea of heavenly beings encircling the throne of God, singing his praise, goes back to the Talmud, where dancing is described as being the principal function of angels. In early Christian times it was supposed that during Divine Service, especially at Mass, the angels were present in the choir participating together with Christ in the performance of the Mystery. Christian iconography has, throughout the centuries, amply illustrated this notion of the singing and dancing angels.

Early fathers of the Church often commented on the dance as a means of worship and of linking the faithful to the angels and blessed souls in Paradise: 'Could there be anything more blessed than to imitate on earth the ring-dance of the angels, and at dawn to raise our voices in prayer and by hymns and songs to glorify the rising Creator?' (St Basil, Bishop of Caesarea, fourth century.)

Symbol and worship

What shapes our lives is a mysterious pattern of movement we cannot actually define, nor do we really understand it; the intellect is not the appropriate tool for apprehending the mysterious dimension of existence, since, like the eye, it can only ever keep a small segment of reality sharply in focus; the synthesis has to be achieved through memory.

The sacred traditions of the world express the realization of man's dependence on the transcendent power, and have sought to establish contact with it through ritual. This contact is thought to be the sole guarantee of the continuation of life. Wherever men have aimed, above all else, at establishing trans-personal values, they have gained a level of development, the quality of which is contained in the essence of achievements of past civilizations, which arise and are renewed always through the creative experiences of a few individuals. Transcendental power articulates myth and ritual as it articulates the shape of plants and trees, the structure of the nervous system, or any other process beyond men's deliberate control. Stylization or abstraction, the portrayal of the power through man-made patterns, equals a reduction of natural, 'realistic' forms to their spiritual essentials, this being equal to a symbolic portrayal of the 'other world'. If symbolism is looked at as a representation of the aspects of the divine it becomes, at the same time, a medium for relating to it.

When a symbol is made to have a finite meaning, as opposed to merely being a paraphrase of the Mysterious, an approximation to Reality, then it becomes an idol. Every important activity in the life of man was initiated by ritual dancing and handed down secretly by the guardians of the tradition after prior ritual preparation. But ritualism, preserved by a priest-caste or power group, who guard the outer form, regardless of changing times or the needs of the developing individual, renders the sacred tradition a mere relic, a fossil. Merely surviving ritual is no longer true, because it is no longer alive; it is just a curious specimen of past human culture. Theology and asceticism add their share to the repression of spontaneous movement; and eventually the dance becomes taboo and is regarded as a dangerous, underground or evil manifestation.

With the progressive development of reflection and the intellect, spontaneity diminishes. Worship shifts increasingly from active physical participation – as in dancing – to contemplative looking-on, and towards a conscious meditative internalization which excludes physical activity and even renders it unnecessary. The mandalic road is trodden or danced imaginatively in contemplative exercises, as an aid for orientating the questing mind to the divine centre in man. 'For the Yogi who hath the perfect divine mandala well defined in his own body, what need is there for the mandala outlined on the ground?' (Y. Evans Wentz, *Tibet's Great Yogi Milarepa*.)

In meditative practices the approach to the divine becomes a psychological turning in a circle around oneself to survey all aspects of oneself; this is to admit that the psyche has just as much reality as the outside world, and that religious experience, which by definition is the appreciation of what is highest, also touches on the deepest levels of the human mind.

Just as early man finds the way beyond himself through a heightening and intensification of his own instinctive responses, the mystic attains to an inner vision of God through his inner resources. Various mystical traditions have evolved their own psychotechnic practices, all based on the insight that man, the microcosm, carries within him the All, and that therefore he may seek and discover it within. These practices rely chiefly on posture and on the rhythmic repetition of sacred formulas; rhythm and sound are regarded as the essence and vehicle of life, as for example, in the Hindu and Buddhist *mantra* and *pranayama* systems, the Hesychast 'prayer of Jesus' or the Islamic *zikr* practice, where breath is regarded as the essence and vehicle of Life.

In myth, the substance of the cosmos is pure sound, which, when transposed into space through rhythm, becomes movement. Ritual chanting aims at reaching the 'sound behind creation', which also lies within the worshipper. Every being who has found his true centre, the 'space of the heart' having been magically transformed into the Centre of the Cosmos, sings and speaks true. The highest Truth being soundless, it is the aim of the mystics 'inner dance' to come face to face with the Silence, the Void beyond the duality of manifest forms. The Japanese practice of facing a bare wall, and the Tibetan exercise of lying on the back and looking into the empty sky, are both aimed at letting the mind reach the state beyond the dissolution of forms, at identifying with the Nothingness which is the All.

Meditative practices slow down the flow of time, and the division between inner and outer disappears. In the moment without duration, opposites are transcended; and it is made possible for the spirit to be encountered anytime or anywhere, rendering the Divine Centre ubiquitous:

> *Now that I see in Mind, I see myself to be the All.*
> *I am in heaven and on earth, in water and in air.*
> *I am in beasts and plants.*
> *I am a babe in the womb and one that is not yet conceived*
> *and one that has been born,*
> *I am present everywhere.*

> *(Upanishads.)*

In meeting the Face that is no face, the interior of man is like the holy of holies in the temple which has no windows. It receives all its light from the Divine.

Within the aureole of timeless Energy, with Asura, demon of ignorance, prostrate underfoot, Shiva, with his head serenely poised, dances the five-fold Dance of Creation, Preservation, Destruction, Veiling and Release. Creation arises from the rhythm of the drum, protection proceeds from the hand of hope, fire effects destruction and transformation, the foot held aloft gives release from bondage, and the promise of Peace is symbolized by the hand pointing to the lifted foot.

All dance-forms having passed away, the Cosmic Dancer remains at the Centre of the Cosmos. Man's search for the still point at the centre of creation eventually finds rest with the dissolution of the 'dream-like forms', when all else is cast out of the heart, so that he alone may abide and dance therein. In the words of Unmai Vilakkam: 'They never see rebirth who behold His mystic dance.'

1 The celestial order is the structuring agent of the human order, of which this mandala of the cosmos in its process of emanation and resorption is the pictorial symbol. Light issues from the point at its centre, the seat of the creator, YHVH, I AM. Penetrating into darkness it creates motion; 'the Spirit of God moved upon the face of the waters'. With motion, eternity enters historical time and infinity becomes structured space. The three outer rings depict the creation of the world and the origin and journey of man. (Genesis, vault of the atrium, St Mark's, Venice, 13th c.)

2 The time and space in which man remembers his creator are sacred by virtue of their power to establish the link with eternity and infinity. The site of ritual worship ensured the encounter with the divine, and divided the place of its manifestation from the fearful, unknown expanse beyond its confines. (Model of sacred enclosure with cult scenes, terracotta, Vounos, Cyprus, c. 2500–2000 BC.)

3 The divinity came to be represented by the shaman or priest, the chosen instrument for the transmission of divine potency. His seat or throne was symbolic of the place of divine manifestation round which the worshippers performed their dance, each thereby relating directly to the source of power and, by revolving round his own axis, becoming himself a centre for divine revelation. Such ceremonies are always related to the death of the old order and the birth of the new, which supersede one another in unending succession. (New Year god dance, Potola Palace, Lhasa, Tibet.)

4 As Sri Nataraja, Lord of the Dance, Shiva dances the five-fold dance of Creation, Veiling, Preservation, Destruction and Release. His aureole of fire emanates from the lotus pedestal; the prostrate Asura, demon of ignorance, lies underfoot. He performs his dance both at the centre of the universe and within the 'burning-ground' of his worshipper's heart, by his grace releasing him from bondage. Shiva's dance is the synthesis of all life experience and an image of all-pervading energy. (Shiva dancing, Bronze, India.)

5 Avalokiteshvara, Bodhisattva of compassion, attends the teaching Buddha Shakyamuni. Countless more Buddhas and Bodhisattvas ascend from his crown in variously changing appearance, filling all the worlds. Ablaze with light, he is omnipresent and all-seeing, his jewel hands embracing all beings. The devotee is brought by his image to an understanding of the law, revealed by the Buddha, of the everpresent glory of all things. (Avalokiteshvara, gouache, Tibet, 18th c.)

6, 7 Matriarchal societies worshipped the feminine as the
Great Goddess, whose body,
the fabric woven by time, contained the whole universe. At
the same time, it was the symbol of all transformative processes, as it united in itself the
elements of earth, water, air
and fire. The seasons of birth,
marriage (union) and death
were sacred to her and celebrated in ritual cults in her
honour. Life was thus worshipped as a single unit, an
insight which found expression in round dances, which
were often of an ecstatic nature. (6 Head of goddess with
round dance of worshippers
on her crown, limestone,
Cyprus, late 6th c. BC; 7 Bell-
shaped goddess with chain of
dancing worshippers, Tanagra,
painted terracotta, Boeotia,
Archaic period.)

8 The creator as the prime mover of the material universe is also the embodiment of the principle of dynamic order. Motion was conceived of as being caused by a vast world of spirits, personifications of various aspects of his power. They direct and order every detail of the world, while singing a continuous song of praise to the creator's glory. (Angels turning the wheels of the universe, miniature, French, 14th c.)

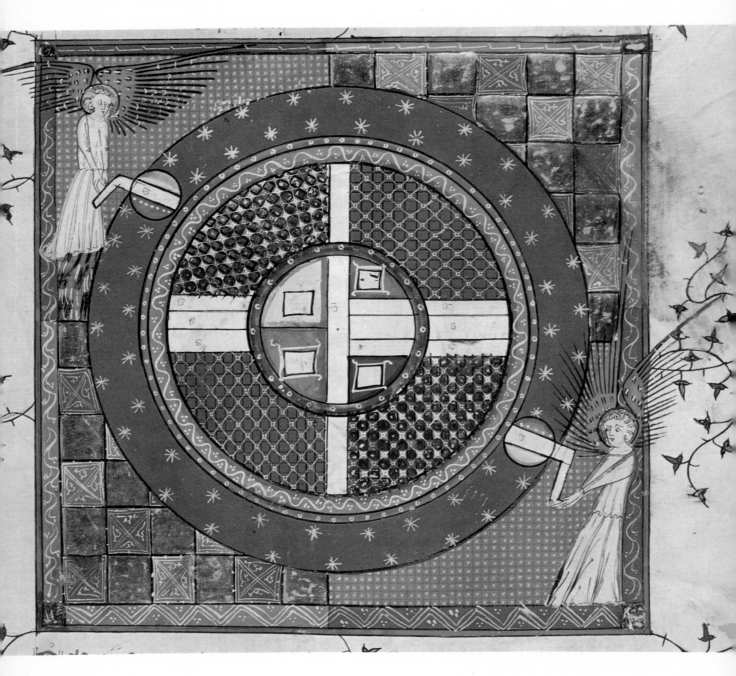

9 God is justice, which is at the root of the principle of order. His *angelos*, or messenger, impartially watches over the dance of the demons of darkness, in their attempt to claim man as their own. Evil, in Christian thought, arises exclusively from the finite, created world and thus comes under divine justice. (Angel of Justice and circling demons, from *Commentarius in Apocalypsin*, 1109.)

10 Spiritual beings, as the essence of all movement and rest, help the life processes towards their fulfilment. They are the link between the worlds of gods and men, and appear to the latter in many different guises. In the *Rig-Veda* the Apsaras, or heavenly nymphs, are connected with the celestial drink *soma*, which incited the god Indra to create the universe. (Nine dancing Apsaras from a temple frieze, Bayon style, India, 12–13th c. AD.)

11 Man's devotion to his god is the chief means of union with him. Chaitanya, 15th-century founder of the Bengali sect of Vaishnavites, preached the doctrine of *bhakti*, the passionate devotion to Krishna as supreme deity. Music, singing and dancing were instrumental in bringing human adoration in accord with divine love. (Vaishnavite devotees dancing, book cover, painted wood, Bengal.)

12 The cosmos in its eternal round begets, preserves, destroys. Tibetan Buddhist iconography depicts the cosmic wheel of life or transmigration, the *Bhavachakramudra*, as being held between the fangs and claws of Shrinmo, demoness of death. In her body the symbols are arranged in three concentric rings. The animals at the centre engender the sinful passions that fetter man to unreality. The ring beyond contains the world of spirits and men. Each separate zone is dominated by a mortal sin. Birth, old age, death and rebirth are depicted in the outermost ring as stages of the eternal life–death cycle. For man to pass beyond it, he has to gain knowledge of the illusory nature of the senses. (Wheel of Life, gouache on cloth, Tibet, late 18th c.)

13 In the great life–death cycle, man celebrates with the New Year the burial of the old and birth of the new, symbol of which is the blazing fire. (Lama New Year dance in celebration of the time of the 'Great Prayer', Sikkim.)

14, 15 The sun surpasses all other planetary gods in the celestial hierarchy. Exalted in the heavens, it sees all and, in consequence, knows all. In India, as Surya, it is the eye of Varuna, in Persia of Ahurmazda; in Greece it is Helios, the eye of Zeus; in Egypt it is that of Ra, and in Islam of Allah. Sun-worship may constitute a religion complete in itself, as in the cult of the Egyptian pharaoh Akhenaton. The invincible character of the sun is compared with that of the moon, which suffers fragmentation before it reaches its monthly three-day phase of disappearance. The sun, on the other hand, does not die in order to descend into the underworld. It can cross the waters without being dissolved; hence the 'death' of the sun always implies rebirth. As symbol of unity, it was worshipped as an image of the ultimate wholeness of man. The experience of attaining to life through death is celebrated ritually by man offering himself or sacrificial gifts to the source of life, in order to promote union. (14 Female figurine invoking the power, painted terracotta, Egypt, *c.* 4000 BC; 15 Akhenaton and Nefertiti offering sacrifice to the sun, relief from the Great Palace, Tel-el-Amarna, 14th c. BC.)

16 According to legend, Amaterasu Omikami, the Great-August-Spirit-Shining-in-Heaven, was one day greatly offended by her brother, the storm-god Susano-O-no-Mikoto. She hid herself in a cave, whereupon darkness fell upon heaven and earth. To entice her forth from her hiding place, eight million spirits from heaven assembled before her cave, erected trees bedecked with jewels, lit fires and danced. The female spirit Uzume performed a particularly wild dance, at which the spirit-gods laughed so uproariously that Amaterasu, curious, peeped out through a chink of her hideout. The gods then held up a mirror before her, and the goddess, drawn out by her own reflection, again gave her light to the world. (The sun-goddess Amaterasu reappearing from her cave, coloured woodcut by Utagawa Kunisada, Japan, 1857.)

17 Seated on the lotus, symbol of ultimate attainment, the divinity's countless attributes are encompassed by the unity of being. (Kan-non statue with one thousand arms, dry lacquer, Nara, Kuzui-Dera, Japan, late 8th c. AD.)

18 The experience of creation in all its aspects came to be personified by manifold deities who embodied the divine activity of which man had become particularly aware and which he strove to imitate. Xochipilli, young Mexican god of flowers, dance, music and love, is one of the thirteen gods who presided over the hours of the day. (Xochipilli, stone, Tlalmanalco, Mexico, Aztec, 14th–15th c.)

19, 20 The incarnation of the divinity in matter and the dissolution of the material form to free the spirit is experienced as circular motion, part of the timeless dance around truth. Angels reveal the plan of the creator and make audible the sound of the cosmos. Their apparition to men is always accompanied by light and music. Their service is the offering of praise to God, the affirmation of the sacred, which for man signifies supreme sacrifice. Angels are therefore always exemplary figures and guides for man. (19 Mystic nativity, painting by Sandro Botticelli, 1500; 20 Souls dancing with angels in Paradise, detail from Last Judgment, painting by Fra Angelico, *c.* 1430–40.)

21, 22 Silence corresponds to the state before creation came into being. Sound, transposed into space, results in motion, both silence and sound being an expression of the mystery. The substance of the cosmos is pure sound, before which the increasing density of matter puts a screen. The ancients regarded music as one of the

most potent forms of magic; to sound the note of creation was to have power over
life and death. Sacred music always attempts to tune in with the sound of creation.
(21 Orpheus charming the animals, mosaic floor, Roman; 22 Krishna playing to
the animals, Indian miniature, Hyderabad, c. 1770.)

23 The measure of man's relationship with the divinity is the extent of his recognition of and participation in its mystery. The task of many semi-divine heroes was to recover a treasure from the 'beyond' for the common world of man. This involved the struggle with the powers guarding it; psychologically, these are personifications of aspects of the hero's own self. (Hercules' fight with Triton, son of Poseidon, with a dance of the Nereids, inside cup, painted terracotta, Greek, 6th c. BC.)

24 The awakening of man is achieved through the mystery of love; the mystical union takes place in silence and in the depth of night. One of the many manifestations of the god Krishna is that of the heavenly dancer. According to legend, he is the chosen beloved of the shepherd girls who, one night at full moon, assembled to perform a round dance with him, the chain being the symbol of the marriage of heaven and earth. (Krishna dancing with the Gopis, embroidered muslin cloth to cover marriage gifts, North India, 18th c.)

25 Many lesser gods of the divine pan-
theon too fulfilled a magic role. Bes,
Egyptian dwarf-god of recreation, had
as his duty to drive away sorrow, scare
off evil spirits and inspire joy. (Bes dancing, panel of the chair of Sitamun, tomb
of Yuia and Thuin, Egypt, c. 1400 BC.)

26 Kali, Hindu goddess of time, presides over the transformation mysteries of death. Her stomach is a void
which can never be filled, her womb gives birth to all
things. The mystery is effected through the consecration of blood from beheaded offerings, which has been
pouring like a river for millennia, returning to its divine
source. Thus, bondage and liberation are equally aspects
of the goddess's power. As the divine mother, after the
destruction of the universe at the end of one great cycle,
Kali gathers the seeds to be sown in the one to come,
when again she brings forth the phenomenal world and
pervades it with her being. (Kali, modern folk-icon,
gouache on cloth, Madhubani, Bihar.)

27 The ancient mysteries were meant to establish a relationship between men and gods. The Egyptian goddess Isis, daughter of Keb, earth, and Nut, sky, was supreme in magical power. Through her union with Osiris she came to be associated with death ritual. Her cult spread to all Roman provinces, where countless shrines existed in her honour. In the Hellenistic mystery cults, which were particularly concerned with the transformation processes of their initiates, the goddess played a central part. (Ceremony of the cult of Isis, wall painting, Pompeii, before AD 79.)

28 The Lares, originally Roman gods of the cultivated fields, came to be worshipped as household gods, where they stood in a special shrine or niche, the Lararium. Usually two of them, as youthful figures with cup and drinking horn, stand on either side of the central figure of Vesta, goddess of the hearth, or some other deity. Prayers and offerings to them were made regularly, and festivals with dancing and games were held in their honour, at which time they were crowned with garlands. (Lararium, wall painting, house of the Vettii, Pompeii, before AD 79.)

29 Gods suppressed become demons; and as a new religion supersedes an older form of worship it relegates the old gods to the realm of the demonic. The Christian Church suppressed indigenous pagan rites as compacts with the devil, to whom all dark, unresolved aspects of creation were ascribed. Yet such rites survive into modern times. The witch-cult worshipped the gods in animal guise and as spirits of nature on mountain sites and forest clearings. The high festivals began in the evening and ended at dawn. (Witches' Sabbath on the Brocken, engraving, Germany, 17th c.)

30 The power of vision is man's strongest motivating and guiding force, the realization of which entails the death of the personal and the birth of the eternal man. The experience of surrender and union is promoted by catharsis or purgation, the redemption of man constituting the release of divine substance in matter. This merging of human and divine love is the essence of every religion. (Union of the soul with God, from *Jerusalem* by William Blake, mezzotint, 1804–20.)

31 Active magic, as an expression of human consciousness and will, is an attempt to break through the cycle of determinacy and establish an independent existence for man. To invoke the power, many rituals contained 'prayers with the body', to an integrating rhythm of chanting and music, linked with ceremonial sacrifice. Such ritual, based on the principle of gradual intensification, with an ecstatic, cathartic climax, promotes the solidarity of life; man acts as the responsible centre of the rite. (Voodoo ceremony, Port-au-Prince, by Gerard Valcin, painting, Haiti, *c.* 1961.)

32 All agricultural communities endeavoured, with the aid of ritual, to heighten the fertility of the earth. Spring and autumn were the times for its celebration in the sacred precinct. Such dances are examples of imitative magic: stamping symbolizes the life-giving movement of the phallus, and hopping symbolizes the growth of seed and plant. (Fertility dance of the Wakamba, Kenya.)

33 The experience of death is at the root of all ritual worship. Yet early man regarded both life and death as an indissoluble unity, death holding the deeper mystery of life in bringing change. All civilizations had elaborate funerary rituals, based on the belief of the resurrection of the dead, the living having the function of aiding this process by executing carefully prescribed movements. In this way, they helped to close the cycle between death and rebirth and assisted the passage of the soul. (Lying-in-state with mourners, geometric amphora, Greece, mid 8th c. BC.)

34 Many cultures know of the idea of death as a
dancer. Impersonations of the dead man were
regarded as a potent means of bringing him back
to life. (Dead man drumming for a dance of dead
warriors, stirrup-spouted jar, Viru Valley, Peru,
Moche culture, *c.* 100 BC–AD 80.)

35, 36 In times of crisis man reacts to a transpersonal situation in a non-personal way. Elaborate funeral rites, as festivals of memory, also offered protection from dread and a means of finding refuge in the fellowship of the community. Through pain and death the soul would rise to divinity. The purpose of such processional dances was to honour and entertain the dead with music, chanting and dances. In Egyptian funeral processions, dances with acrobatic movements and varied rhythms were accompanied by the clapping of hands and waving of branches. At the tomb itself, before the statue of the dead, the dances for the *ka*, the soul of the deceased, took on a more solemn character. Many funeral dances are chain dances, performed with interlinked arms around the bier or funeral pyre. They are protective in nature, and symbolic of the unity of life and death. The ritual movement follows the direction of the sun's course. (35 Acrobatic dancers, wall painting, tomb of Mehu, Saqqara, Egypt, *c.* 2500–2350 BC; 36 Funeral dance, wall painting, tomb of Ruvo, Naples, Etruscan, 4th c. BC.)

37, 38 The mask, equivalent to the chrysalis, fosters de-personalization and identification with the chosen deity. In dancing, man imitates the god's movements and
thus achieves union with him. As priest, man in ritual worship becomes the symbol
for the ordered manifestation of the transcendental power, through whom it reveals
its claims. (37 Dancing priest, Campeche, Mexico, solid clay. *c*. AD 700–1000;
38 Dancer with bird mask, terracotta, North West Coast, Mexico, Colima style,
AD 300–1000.)

39 'Thus all Israel brought up the ark of the covenant of the Lord with shouting, and with sound of the cornet, and with trumpets, and with cymbals, making a noise with psalteries and harps. . . . And David danced before the Lord with all his might, and David was girded with a linen ephod. . . . And it came to pass, as the ark of the covenant of the Lord came to the city of David, that Michal the daughter of Saul looking out of the window, saw king David dancing and playing: and she despised him in her heart' (I Chronicles 15: 28; II Samuel 6: 14; I Chronicles 15: 29). St Augustine describes David's dance as 'the mysterious figuration of the sacred harmony of all sounds and gestures'. (David dancing before the ark of the Lord, miniature from a *Bible Moralisée*, France, 13th c.)

40 Dancing and incantation in memory of God, the 'Beloved', has a place in Islamic mysticism. In some Dervish orders it became a major form of worship. 'The dance opens a door in the soul to divine influence. . . . The dance is good when it arises from the remembrance of the Beloved. Then each waving sleeve has a soul in it' (Sa'adi, d. 1291). (Dervishes dancing, miniature from the *Kamsah* of Amir Khusran, Persia, 1485.)

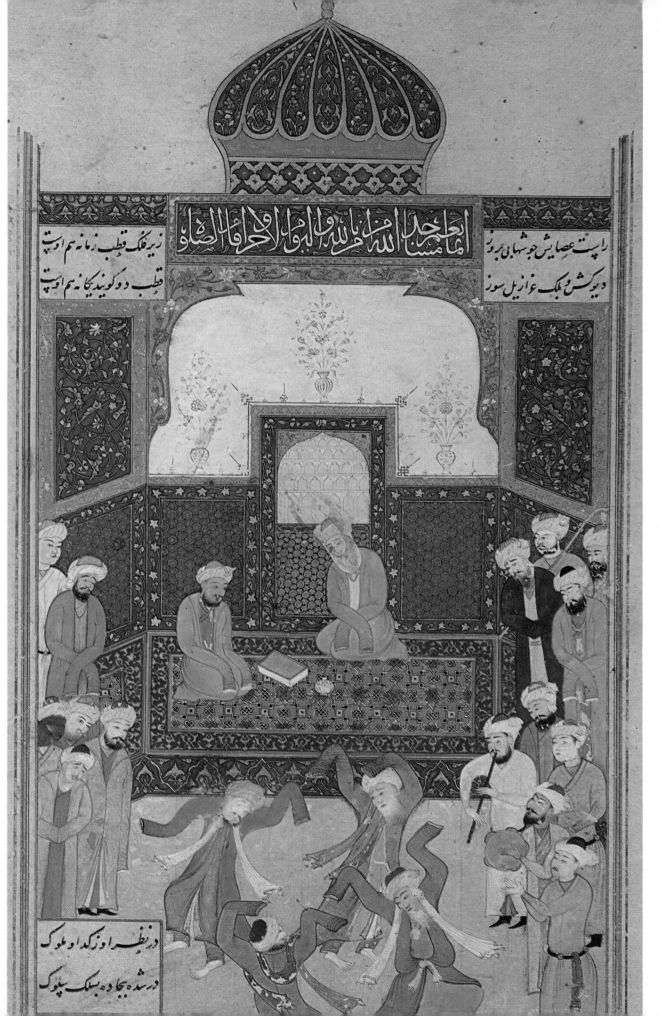

41 As the dance is one of the most ancient forms of magic, representations of dance ritual can be found among the cultural relics of even the early hunters and planters. Subterranean and mountain caves, as the womb of the Great Goddess, were the earliest sites for worship. The dance, being a ritual metamorphosis, often calls for the use of the mask both to facilitate and to conceal the transformation of the dancer into a god. (Masked figures in a round dance, rock-painting, Sefar, Tassili n'Ajjer, Algeria.)

42, 43 Ecstatic liberation of the self was sought in Dionysian dances. Dionysus, or Bacchus, was honoured with orgiastic rites which, like the dream, offer a sense of freedom from the limitations of the body. Dancing played a crucial role as an expression of spontaneous seizure. Ecstasy is akin to sacrifice, making the vessel of the body empty and fit for the god to enter – just as he dwells in other manifestations of nature, in stones, rivers or trees. Dionysus' sacred madness took hold of women, who left their homes, roaming around in wild places in a state of intoxication. By contrast, Apollo's spiritual significance is identical with that of the sun and the light of consciousness. He too is depicted singing to the lyre and dancing. At Delphi the cults of Dionysus and Apollo came to be reconciled, when the statues of both gods stood facing one another. The seer Melampus, devoted to both gods, is said to have tamed the Dionysian movement by taking the strongest youths and making them chase the raving Bacchantic women from the mountains amid cries and dancing. (42 Boy and girl dancing at a festival in honour of Apollo, volute krater, Taranto, c. 410 BC; 43 Bacchanalian dance, wall painting, Villa Pamphilii, Rome, 1st c. AD.)

45 The gods in all their different manifestations rule the lives of man. Illness and death are considered to be caused by superhuman powers, and need to be countered by invoking those powers or aspects of the god which rule the good, life-giving forces. Exorcistic dance rites are carried out for people afflicted with illness or psychic disturbance. (Boota dance, South Kanara, Mysore, India.)

44 Women were often exclusively in charge of seasonal rituals, as is still the case in this dance, where the women welcome spring with chanting and music. (Spring dance of the Santal, North-east India.)

46 The shaman's function was to mediate between the world of spirits and the members of his tribal community, who saw him as the ancestor's specially chosen mouthpiece for prophecy and as an instrument of healing. Both these functions were vital for the tribe, for which the shaman was the medicine-priest. The shaman's encounter with the spirits, both good and evil, when acted out, took on a very dramatic form. (Shaman dancing with spirits, miniature from the *Fatik Album* of Ustat Mehmed Siyal Kalem, Turkey, 15th c.)

48 Religious dance ritual, with its central focus of communion with the deity, came in time to be absorbed into the vast heritage of folk custom. The Tree of Life, as world axis linking heaven and earth, and pathway for the shaman's ascent to the abode of the ancestor, survives as the May-tree or Maypole. It is often richly decorated, serving as the centre for the villagers' annual round dance, and is part of a now thoroughly secularized type of seasonal entertainment. (May dance, painting by Pieter Bruegel the younger, 1634.)

47 At the *haloa*, Greek festivals of harvest and vintage, the gods of earth and vegetation were honoured with dances. The state of intoxication through wine was worshipped as the epiphany of the divinity. During such times man participates for a moment in the mode of being that is attributed to the gods. (Vintage dance, terracotta antefix, Myrene, Asia Minor, Roman period.)

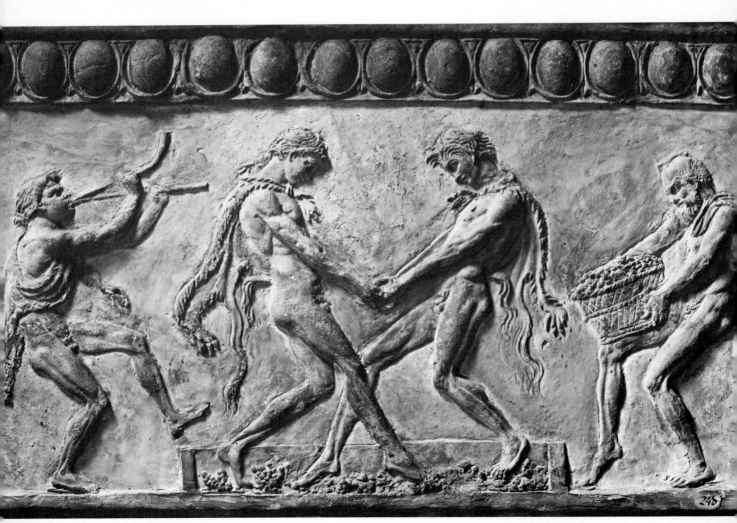

49, 50 Initiation into the secret knowledge of a community, which reflects its understanding of the laws of creation, presents itself to the neophyte essentially as an experience of death and rebirth. Through initiation rituals at the decisive points of birth, puberty, marriage and death, the neophyte's insight deepens and is made conscious. At the tribal level, the guardians of the threshold test the initiate before he can become a full member of the community. In the Hellenistic mystery cults, initiation into higher levels of life was preceded by an experience of darkness and bewilderment. Initiation is symbolic of the conquest of self and the liberation of the divine essence within. (49 Puberty initiation dance of the Karaja, Brazil; 50 Initiation ceremony, wall painting, House of Mysteries, Pompeii, *c.* AD 50.)

51, 52 Man, who learned to dance from the animals, imitated their sounds and movements, in an attempt to be like the adored divinity which dwelt within them. The cranes, in their mating dance, raise their wings, lift their feet, sink their heads into their breasts and lift them again, while shuffling round in a circle. They accompany their movements with irregular rhythmic sounds, part song, part cry. (51 Cranes dancing; 52 Girls of the Watussi dancing the dance of the Crowned Cranes, Zaïre.)

54 Within the walls of the temple court, rows of men gather at night round a burning torch to celebrate the Ketjak, or monkey-trance dance. It is primarily a dance of exorcism, based on a story from the *Ramayana*. The sounds and movements together create a strong union of mood to drive away evil. During the climax of the dance, the chorus, crouching at the feet of their leader, gathers into two semi-circles which face one another and, with powerful cries and wild gestures, drive away the demons of night, after which they fall back into silence. (Monkey-trance dance, Bali.)

53 Commemorative worship of the tribe's ancestor was always accompanied by dancing. Man's return to the ancestor, that is, to his own origin, depends on establishing intimate contact with him. Such commemorative dancing around the totem was very common among the North American Indians. (Watercolour by John White, Virginia, 1585–93.)

55 In medieval Europe, during public festivals, especially at Christmas, bands of men and women would gather, in masks and fancy dress, processing through the streets and serenading outside houses where festivities were held. Mumming, probably a survival of the Roman custom of masquerading during the Saturnalia, is an example of religious ritual entering the common heritage of the folk and becoming mere entertainment. (Mummers, miniature from the *Roman de Fauvel*, France, 14th c.)

56 In a cosmic sense, war concerns the struggle of light against darkness, good against evil. War is also the means of reinstating the original order of the creator. This is synonymous with the sacrifice of diversity to attain unity, facilitated by ritual orientation, where the terrestrial centre becomes the symbolic visual centre of the cosmos. (War dance of the 'mud men', Goroka, Papua–New Guinea.)

57 In ritual dance the warrior's role is that of defending the centre against the chaotic forces which threaten the harmony of balance from outside. In Islamic sacred tradition, war between men is the 'Little War' in relation to the 'Great Holy War', which is fought to liberate man from the enemies within. (Warrior dance, New Guinea.)

58 In the battle to be fought for the establishment of Dharma in the world, that is, for the order which supports the universe, the god Krishna acts as the charioteer of his disciple Arjuna, who, realizing the truth revealed to him by the god, is able to fight for the universal goal without thinking of personal ends. (Krishna and Arjuna driving to the battle of Kurukshetra, from the Hindu epic *Mahabharata*.)

59 The sun, as the source of life, is at the centre of many dance rituals. It is often associated with the Tree of Life, whose crown or fruit it forms. By encircling the sun-pole with the solar symbol at its top, the worshipper gave it magical aid, helping it along its path. The main times for sun-worship were the solstices and equinoxes. (Dakota sun dance, watercolour on paper by Short Bull, chief of the Oglala, Dakota and Sioux, *c.* 1930.)

60 All marriage ritual is ultimately symbolic of
the life-generating union of heaven and earth. The
conjunction of opposites ensures both fertility and
longevity. In many ceremonies the man and
woman are dressed in the robes of king and queen
and wear ritual crowns, symbol of union. (Zulu
marriage dance, South Africa.)

61 The Tree of Life, as the world axis linking above with below,
continues to hold its promise. Symbol of the unity of all life, and
thus of immortality, it is at the centre of the round dance of creation. (Wish-granting tree, gouache on cloth, Tibet, 18th c.)

*Documentary illustrations
and commentaries*

Sacred Space

Man has always experienced the space around him as an epiphany of the divine, the circling aeons tracing the life and death of the world. The symbol for the all-seeing, all-knowing god has always been the starry night sky, while the zodiac mirrors the destiny of the world and man. The Babylonians believed that the zodiac dances a ring-dance to the harmony of the heavenly spheres, which is reflected in the divinely ordered yearly round of the processes of transformation on earth (1). In the Christian idiom, it is the Logos, ministered to by a host of angelic beings, which creates the worlds: 'In the beginning was the Word, and the Word was with God, and the Word was God' (2). In space the countless aspects of the Divine reveal themselves and come to be worshipped as separate divinities (3). The division of space follows from the time-pattern traced by the movement of the planets, as reflected in the changes of season, the growth and decay of vegetal life and the ages of man. Man, by his nature, participates in all cosmic events and is inwardly and outwardly interwoven with them, mankind as a whole having common instincts of imagination and action. With time, the experience of the surrounding universe becomes transformed into ritual worship, which signifies man's response to the demands of manifest power.

The oldest sacred structures known, the megalithic sanctuaries, were modelled on the celestial pattern (5). Sacred space is the intermediary zone between cosmos, as structured, man-created space, and chaos, the formless, unknown void, it becomes the established locality for the encounter with the divine. It always consists of an inner sanctuary and an outer temple or area, and the structures are based on the concepts of orientation and level, indicated by the central point, radial axes and circumference.

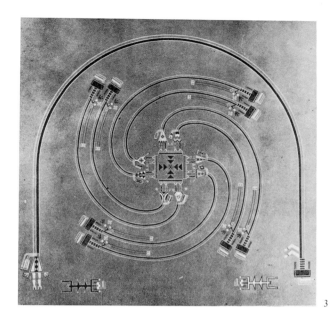

3

4

The spiral, as the schematic image of the evolution of the universe, traces the movement between unity, symbolized by the central point, and multiplicity, encompassed by the outer circle. One of its symbolic attributes is dynamic power, as exemplified in the expansion of stellar nebulae or the contraction of whirlpools. The earliest spatial symbols are very elementary; with time they become filled with more and more sense-content. The oldest forms, indicating ritual movement, are the meander and the circle. Wavy lines within concentric circles, which develop into elaborate mazes, denote searching.

1 Model of the solar system.
2 Angel holding the scroll of heaven. (Wall-painting in the Church of the Saviour, Kariye Çamii, Istanbul, *c.* 1310.)
3 Design of whirling rainbows. (North American Indian sand-painting.)
4 Cosmic diagram of the world-mountain as the centre of the world, surrounded by the world ocean, the four corners of the world and magic symbols. (Back of a marriage mirror, bronze, T'ang Dynasty, AD 713–42, Seattle Art Museum.)
5 Stone circle, oriented to the sun's path. (Arbor Low, England.)

5

6

The circle itself contains the ideas of incorporating, giving, receiving and excluding. As emblem of the mystery, the labyrinth protects the sacred centre, and at the same time affords initiation to him who ventures along its winding pathway, the symbol of obstructed penetration into the inner sanctuary. Many initiatory temples of later civilizations, notably in Egypt, but especially in Greece and the Hellenistic world, were labyrinthine in construction. With the labyrinth the earliest dance forms have a close connection. They are related to states of ecstasy, round and whirling dances being the purest kind of dance devotion because of their strict emphasis on the centre and the creation of inner space. In sacred time, the barriers of chronological time break down, and there is a reversion towards the origin, which is identical with the centre, as the model for all development. Sacred time links personal fate with that which transcends it. Round dances are primordial, potent and universal. The Greek *emmeleia* are choral dances in which the chorus with their leader move from circle to spiral, snake line, meander, double circle and chain. The close relation of the dancers with one another, holding hands or hooking arms, forces everyone into the same rhythm and stride (6–8).

7

The square, as the symbol of the earth, is encircled by the worshipper in processional dances. Circling the square emphasizes the spiritual unity of the material world which manifests in opposites (9). The path which leads to the sanctuary is sacred. Along it the ritual procession passes with chanting and music, as a preparatory rite for the holy office within the temple (10). The ritual ploughing of the first furrow is an ancient annual ceremony, whereby the earth is opened and penetrated for fertility. Tools and implements used in the rite were sacred as endowed with magic powers (11).

6 Open round dance with lyre player. (Painted terracotta, Palaikastro, Crete, late Minoan period III, 1400–1100 BC, Heraklion Museum.)

7 Round dance with musician in the centre. (Terracotta, Boeotian, 6th c. BC, Kestner-Museum, Hanover.)

8 Round dance. (Andonara, Celebes.)

9 'Illumined is the Ka'aba by walking round it, while the other houses of man remain in darkness . . . And he [who is circling round the Ka'aba] should appear to himself during this rite like the angels round the throne of God' (the Sufi Futuhat). (Muslims circling the Ka'aba, Mecca, engraving, 1803, British Museum, London.)

10 Procession with musicians and impersonations of the gods. (Drawing after a mural painting, Maya, Bonampak, Mexico, *c.* AD 700, Peabody Museum, Harvard University.)

11 Ploughing the first furrow. (Roman relief, Museo Archeologico, Aquileia.)

The centre enshrines the young or new-born god. It is the task of the warrior priests to protect his life against destruction or dismemberment (15). In ancient Greece, commanders in battle were called 'principal dancers', and, according to Socrates, 'the men who dance best are the best warriors'.

'When the aulos had given the signal for the attack, rhythm and sounds determined the motions of the warriors. And indeed, they have achieved by their ordering themselves according to music, that they always excel above all others in battle' (Lucian on the martial customs of Thessaly) (13).

By implication, the sacred site for worship is an image of the world; it is the locality 'where every where and every when is focused' (Dante). As such, it needs protection from the chaotic forces of outer darkness. This conflict is often ritually enacted as the battle between the cosmic forces of darkness and light (14). The warrior-priests went into battle to fight in the name of their god—the tribe's or nation's enemy always being regarded as the enemy of the god they have adopted. With encircling, marching dances a magic ring is drawn round the sanctuary, so that nothing may escape from it or penetrate into its interior (16). In Rome, during the annual festivals held in honour of Mars, the priest caste of the *Salii* held armed processions in the streets. Under their leader, the *praesul*, they executed intricate weaving movements to a three-step, stamping heavily and loudly clanging their shields and lances. Halting at all altars and temples in town, they accompanied their dancing by an ancient litany.

12

13

12 Dance of the Corybantes. (Greek relief, Vatican Museums.)
13 Greek phalanx led into battle by an aulos-player. (Oenochoe, painted terracotta, Corinth, late 7th c. BC, Villa Giulia, Rome.)
14 Staff dance of dancers representing sun and moon. (Java.)
15 The Kouretes with their pyrrhic dance protect the infant Zeus against the pursuit of Chronos (Saturn). From Crete the pyrrhic dance spread to Sparta and other Greek provinces. (Campanian relief, Louvre, Paris.)
16 Round dance by thirteen soldiers. (Painted terracotta cup, Athens, c. 775–750 BC, Antikensammlungen, Munich.)

Just as before going into battle the warriors consecrated themselves to their god, so the dancer within the temple was sacred
to the divinity. By dancing, the worshipper established and
defined his relationship with his god. In annual dance ritual there
took place an attunement to seasonal change that re-established
the bond between the earth and the sky, the dancer with his body
traversing and moulding space.

The Early Christian Easter ritual celebrated the rebirth of the
Saviour-Sun with dancing and music: 'Beg and pray to Christ,
that thy life may be lived in Christ. That by the Easter festival
thou mayst be awakened and come out of the labyrinth' (from
a stone of a labyrinth, preserved in Lyons museum) (18, 19).
Dancing, as a means of affirming creation and of worshipping
its creator is celebrated in the Gnostic 'Hymn of Jesus': 'To each
and all it is given to dance . . . He who joins not in the dance
mistakes the event . . . Thou shouldst understand and understanding say: Glory to Thee, Father! Amen.'

17 Interior of Hagia Sophia, Istanbul. (Lithograph from G.
Fossati's *Aya Sofia, Constantinople, as recently restored*, 1852.)
18 Labyrinth in Chartres Cathedral. (Drawing from J. Gail-
habaud's *L'Architecture du Vᵉ au XVIIᵉ siècle*, 1858.)
19 Labyrinth in Reims Cathedral. (Drawing, Bibliothèque
Nationale, Paris.)

17

18

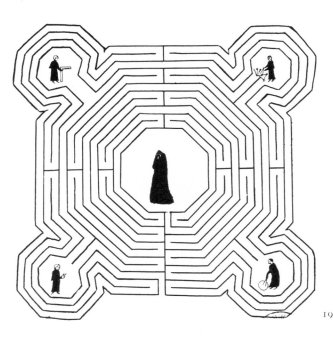

19

20

Gesture and ritual

Man's encounter with the gods constitutes the basis for all experience. In his rituals, which express his relationship with the divine, man expresses his most deeply rooted fears and hopes. Ritual behaviour shows the application of human insight and emotion to non-human phenomena; and a community's rituals provide the external link with the transcendental power. Ritual dance, which is initially simply a mimed response to experience and an imitation of movement observed in nature, later develops into ritual drama, the account of the mythic origins of the universe, the gods and man. The language of ritual gesture is universal, encompassing the whole range of human experience. The most potent of experiences, those of awe, surrender and ecstasy, dissolve in turn in the experience of attaining the centre, when the expression through motion is transcended. Ritual gestures blend spontaneous movement with gestures canonized by tradition and given a specific form and style, prescribed to the last detail. Just as an experience may vary in intensity and quality, so the application of ritual models as stereotypes of human behaviour is endlessly variable. And yet all ritual is universal and timeless in that it is essentially concerned with the offering of praise to the deity, with *the affirmation of creation as it is.*

20 Japanese priestesses at prayer on the south shore of Hateruma Island. (Japan.)

21 A Muslim at prayer.

In the transmission of ritual, memory is the single most important factor, all occasions of ritual worship being festivals of remembrance of the divinity. The way towards an encounter with the gods leads into the past; it is the way to the origin which ultimately transcends the historical condition and all created forms. In an attempt to share the destiny and attributes of his god, man strives, above all, to become like him, anticipate his wishes, obey his orders and imitate his attributes. This, for man, involves transformation and transcendence of himself.

Gestures, as imitative magic, have the capacity of transmitting power and of drawing it unto the worshipper. Whatever their function in a given ritual, their significance is always psychological, in that they release energy and transform it; when included in dance, they are given special emphasis through rhythm and music. Ritual acts are often preceded by elaborate secret preparations, involving ablution, abstinence from certain foods and drinks and from sexual intercourse, seclusion, vigils and periods of intense prayer: in this way the unity of purpose is enhanced by a unity of effort in which the whole community has a share.

During the process of ritual worship the body becomes the receptacle for the divine power which manifests and expresses itself through it, thereby transforming it. The dance, in this way, is the art of portraying the spiritual, changing natural man into cultural man. The organized rite is an endeavour to keep the individual and the group in constant touch with the divine; and only much later, in established world religion, does the dance, as a means of worship, recede into the background in favour of the spoken word.

22 Muslims at prayer in sacred enclosure, Egypt.

22

23 Figurine with arms raised in worship. (Terracotta, Egyptian, predynastic, Übersee-Museum, Bremen.)
24 Aboriginal ceremony on the banks of the Umbakumba Creek. (Bark painting, Australia.)

23

24

25 The times and seasons when rituals were performed, were sacred as times particularly propitious for the manifestation of the deity. (Men of the Hapaee tribe at a ritual at night, engraving by W. Sharp after J. Webber, *The Voyages of Captain Cook*, 1777.)

26 To free the spirit from the sluggish matter that keeps it in bondage is the endeavour of the revivalist cult of the Shakers. (Shakers near Lebanon, lithograph by N. Currier, The Harry T. Peters Collection, Museum of the City of New York.)

26

27

28

29

In all postures of prayer man is present in an impersonal way, transcending his individuality. Devotional movement alludes to situations and relationships of which the most eloquent are the gestures of invocation, the appeal to the deity to reveal itself (20–28, 30, 31). Gestures of invocation are equalled in intensity by those of rejoicing and thanksgiving (29, 32, 33). The actual encounter with the god, with the mystery, is the centre of the rite.

30

27 Sacred dance with, probably, the goddess descending in the centre. (Bezel of a gold signet ring, Isopata, near Knossos, *c.* 1500 BC, Heraklion Museum, Crete.)
28 Invocation of the spirit of Kali, by a dancer impersonating her, performed in temples dedicated to Bhagavatis, the female aspect of god, before the Tiyyattu Dance. (Kerala, India.)
29 Harvesters in a procession of thanksgiving. (Detail of the Harvesters' Vase, black steatite rhyton, Palace of Hagia Triada, Crete, *c.* 1550–1500 BC, Heraklion Museum, Crete.)
30 Ritual gestures of Devil Dancers in costume. (Sri Lanka.)

32

31

31 Ritual dance by two girls. (Metope from the temple of Hera, Paestum, late 4th c. BC, Paestum Museum.)
32 Dancers before an offering. Traditional ceremony at the beginning of a performance of the Baris Poleng. (Pagoeten, Bali.)
33 Durga Puja, performed in a temple in honour of the goddess Devi's victory over the giant Doorg. (Watercolour by Sewak Ram, India, *c.* 1807.)

33

The animal as ancestor

For early man the natural universe was filled with power, which he experienced as having quite concrete reality: all things to him were the carriers of a soul, either benevolent or harmful. This power, as the spirit or life of things, forever calling him into service and constituting the 'Great Unknown', he visualized in the form of gods and demons. By this power all aspects of nature are connected and participate with one another. The part stands for the whole; that is, any single aspect of the divinity may represent him in his totality.

Surrounded by these mysterious forces, early man was activated, by every strong impression, to respond, imitate, recreate. He felt it his task to influence and pacify these powers; this, combined with the innate tendency of man to serve and adore that which he experiences to be the stronger and greater, laid the foundation for all ritual worship to come.

The tribe's ancestor was identified with a particular totem animal (usually one that the tribe hunted), and became the carrier of all the forces of nature. Man saw it as his task to imitate the god's destiny and attributes in ritual dance (35, 37). Prehistoric cave-paintings show man, clothed in animal skins and masks, dancing and celebrating the animal's strength, following his prey and appeasing the animal's spirit when he had killed it (34, 36). Vestiges of such ancient ritual behaviour may still be observed in the ceremonies of the North American Indians, the Eskimos and the Siberian Ostyaks. One of the oldest rituals, connected with the ancestral god, is eating the meat of the sacrificial animal, which is to partake of the meal of the deity, whose blessings are thereby assimilated by the worshipper. Animal dances make use of rhythmic stamping and leaping movements, and are accompanied by sounds appropriate to the animal, by nature sounds and the clapping of hands.

34 Masked sorcerer. (Drawing after a prehistoric cave-painting, Les Trois Frères, Arriège.)
35 Dance of ancestor worship. (Vietnam.)
36 Dancer with animal mask. (North West Mexico, Colima style, AD 300–1000, Stendahl Galleries.)
37 Aboriginal dancers imitating the ancestral spirit. (Australia.)
38 Love dance of scorpions.

34

35

36

37

38

The role of the priest

The powerlessness of man-made magic, when faced with the transcendent reality, always points to the deity as the superior being in relation to man. To bring the human order into accord with the divine, to be in constant touch with the mystery and make manifest the sacred, to celebrate the whole of life as a sacrament, needed men with special powers. The divinity (39, 40) came to be represented on earth by the tribal chief, the shaman or priest, who concentrated in his person such powers as enabled him to come face to face with the mystery. Often he was the only member of the community permitted to make contact with the deity and represent it in the sacred dances. In these dances in honour of the god there takes place a complete identification with the deity and its powers (41, 43, 45, 46). As healer, teacher and prophet (47–49), the priest is the chosen vehicle for divine office and revelation. It is his task to interpret to the community the god's attributes, his demands and blessings. As intermediary between gods and men, the priest stands for the ordered, the prophet and medicine-man for the occasional, manifestation of power.

39

39 Images of the gods outside the crater of Rano Raraku. (Easter Island, 1100 (?)–*c*. 1680.)
40 The priest-king Quetzalcóatl as the wind god Ehécatl. (Mexican body stamp, Texcoco, before 1521.)
41 Warriors dancing round their priests during a ceremony of instilling courage. (Engraving from A. Picart's *Cérémonies et coutumes religieuses*, 1735, Victoria and Albert Museum, London.)
42 The gods being honoured with music and chanting by an Aztec orchestra. (Miniature from *Codex Magliabecchi*, facsimile, 1904.)
43 Eagle-headed deities represented on either side of the Sacred Tree by their priests. (Assyrian relief, Nimrud, *c*. 884 BC, British Museum.)

40

41

42

43

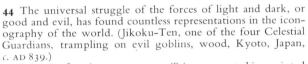

44

45

46

44 The universal struggle of the forces of light and dark, or good and evil, has found countless representations in the iconography of the world. (Jikoku-Ten, one of the four Celestial Guardians, trampling on evil goblins, wood, Kyoto, Japan, *c.* AD 839.)

45 Priest performing a ceremony. (Stirrup-spouted jar, painted terracotta, Moche Culture, Peru, before *c.* AD 800, Linden-museum, Stuttgart.)

46 Dance worship at a tree shrine. (Gold signet ring, Mycenae, National Museum, Athens.)

47 The priest in his function of transmitting the power of life and regeneration. (The relics of St Dionysius carried in procession over a paralysed woman, Island of Zante.)

48 In ceremonies of healing and exorcism, the sick man is placed in the centre of the cosmic mandala. (Blessing with an eagle wand during a Navajo ceremony, Arizona.)

49 The shaman, as healer and prophet, communicates the message of the ancestral spirit to his tribe in a state of trance. (Shaman dancing with his drum, the symbol of the universe, engraving from Nicolaes Witsen's *Noord en Oost Tartarye*, 1705.)

47

48

49

50

Release and ecstasy

The encounter with the divinity in ecstatic dance rites implies the identification of man with his god to the extent where he is completely overwhelmed, or 'possessed'. If he expresses himself in this state, it means that it is the god who does so through him. Some cults made systematic use of music and dancing with the exclusive aim of achieving the ecstatic state, where ordinary consciousness is flooded, and dammed-up emotional forces are released. The experience of rapture, of being beside oneself, is synonymous with being filled with a power greater than one's own. The prerequisite for such an experience is the worshipper's capacity to surrender, to let go of all that he knows and clings to for support. Such a release of energy expresses itself in dance movements which are spontaneous and dynamic.

Every festival of rejoicing and thanksgiving, as in fertility rites (51) or New Year celebrations (50), includes elements of the ecstatic. Historically, one of the best-documented ecstasy cults is that connected with the worship of the god Dionysus. Rituals in his honour included orgiastic rites, the sacrifice of animals,

51

52

wine-drinking and trance dances, which continued until the dancers collapsed with exhaustion. Self-flagellation, to the point where the body becomes insensitive to pain, and man transcends the awareness of his physical limitations, often precedes the state of trance and the release of ecstasy (52, 54).

The ecstasy of wild whirl and leap dances is accompanied by strong changing rhythms and powerful cries, which convey the excess of emotion, as opposed to introverted mystical dances which make use of dark, aspirated humming sounds and mellow, tuneful music. Strong rhythms effect change, and dances with exciting rhythms heighten the feeling of togetherness, instil courage and break down emotional and mental barriers. Ecstasy cults are dynamic, and because of their strong impact they are contagious. Consequently, whether inside or outside a current religion, they tend to be suppressed and their exponents persecuted, as constituting a potential or actual political danger to the established system.

50 Dancers in procession during the Holi festival. Lucknow. India. (Watercolour, c. 1800–10, India Office Library, London.)
51 Farmers celebrating the harvest. (Japan.)
52 Maenads worshipping Dionysus. (Stamnos, painted terracotta, c. 420 BC, Museo Nazionale, Naples.)
53 Dionysus in frenzy, tearing apart a kid. The maenads. worshipping the god, danced with covered arms, which they moved like wings. (Vase, British Museum, London.)
54 Flagellants. (Woodcut, 1493.)
55 Voodoo dance ceremony. (Haiti.)

53

54

55

Sacrifice, death, rebirth

'And in dying is all; and there is no other way to life and true peace' (Thomas à Kempis, *The Imitation of Christ*). The great cycle of life, from birth to death and new birth, is at the very core of every type of worship. Sacrificial formulae were necessary to maintain and safeguard the order of the universe; and therefore gestation and birth, marriage and death, were repeated ritually, symbolically, as the phases of life which hold the key to a higher form of existence. Such new life had to be earned, by offering up to the deity what one treasured most. Rites of rebirth rely strongly on the rendering of sacrifice to release power; and this power, the new life, is proportionate in intensity to the degree of surrender. In this way, sacrifice is the 'strait gate' which leads unto life.

Historically, the sacrificial act has undergone a long development, from human and blood sacrifice to the mystic's renunciation of the claims of the ego. The fundamental insight is that death is the source of life and the resurrection of matter, and that life, in order to continue, must feed on life (50–60). In religious terms, this means the periodic self-sacrifice of the deity for the sake of the greater Life (72). For the individual this experience is verified in the words of the apostle Paul: 'It is sown a natural body; it is raised a spiritual body.'

59

56 Fruit sacrifice. (Stucco relief from House of the Priestess of Isis, Museo delle Terme, Rome.)
57 Sacrifice to Ceres. (Wall-painting, Pompeii, before AD 79, Museo Nazionale, Naples.)
58 Bacchantes leading a bull to sacrifice. (Roman relief, Vatican Museums.)
59 The sacrifice of Isaac. (Tapestry, c. 1120, Cathedral Treasury, Halberstadt, Germany.)
60 Human sacrifice, Chichén Itzá. (Drawing from a Maya disc of sheet gold by Tatiana Prouskouriakoff, courtesy of the Carnegie Institution of Washington.)

60

Rituals of initiation, as part of every form of worship, have as their aim the release of the neophyte from the past and thereby prepare him for the future. This often involved arduous and painful procedures, including castigation and mutilation of the body (61). At Eleusis, the myths that incorporated the secret knowledge of the cult were shown to the initiates in the form of dance ritual (62). The ancient mystery institutions had two main grades of initiation. In the lower one were shown the mysteries of generation or physical birth, in the higher one the mystery of regeneration and spiritual birth and life. The symbolism of marriage stood for final union. To meet the transformation in nature with a transformation of self was the basic precept of initiation ritual; transubstantiation was its essential aim.

61 Dance of the myth of creation at an Aborigine boy's circumcision ceremony. (Yirrkalla district, Northern Territory, Australia.)
62 The soul in darkness, broken down under the burden of the *stauros*. The beloved, the god of the past, symbolized by the phallus, is now veiled. (Young initiate with *stauros* and veiled phallus, Villa of Mysteries, Pompeii, *c.* AD 50.)
63 Death represented as a devouring monster. The terrifying Unknown is always portrayed full face, with large, dominating eyes. (Ritual drama, Bali.)
64 The ultimate sacrifice is voluntary self-sacrifice of the worshipper. (Kris dance, Bali.)

Dances at funerals were rebirth rather than mourning rites, and were based on the belief of the continuation of life beyond death (69). Plato (*Laws*, Book 12) describes the burial of an Athenian king, where the bier was preceded by a host of youths and maidens, carrying wreaths and branches. They danced slowly and solemnly to the accompaniment of music. After them, in procession, came priests from various temples, clothed in different robes. Funeral dances were representative of the sun's energy, symbol of life which, although suffering a temporary eclipse by its descent below the horizon, emerges to revitalize the living creatures. Thus, dances of death, which are frequently labyrinthine or circular in character, are essentially dances of rebirth, the union of the two worlds being made evident by the relation of the danced ring with its pivotal point at the centre.

On the island of Delos, no sacrifice was offered without song and dance. In the Geranos dance, performed at night time in memory of Theseus and his wanderings in the Cretan labyrinth, the chorus of seven youths and seven maidens, holding hands, followed their leader round an altar of Aphrodite. The youths chanted a solemn hymn, while the maidens moved round the image of the deity in silence (67). The Cretan labyrinth has found its way into the early medieval Gothic cathedrals. Theseus was identified with Christ, who, at Easter re-emerged triumphantly from the jaws of hell. In celebration of his death and resurrection the Pelota dance (cf. p.27) was annually performed on a labyrinthine floor in the cathedral of Auxerre.

Death, rebirth and the soul's wanderings on the road to God are celebrated in the ritual of the Mevlevi order of Dervishes. The symbolic centre, seat of life, which is both within and without the worshipper, is circumscribed in the dance and thereby called upon to reveal itself (68).

65 Death as the dancer invites the living, irrespective of age and class, to give themselves to him, dancing. (Dance of death, wall-painting in the church of la Chaise-Dieu, Haute-Loire.)
66 Mourners. (Etruscan stele, 5th c. BC, Museo Baracco, Rome.)
67 Theseus with Athenian youths and maidens in the Geranos dance. (Detail of the François Vase, made by Ergomitos and painted by Kleitas, painted terracotta, *c.* 570 BC, Museo Archeologico, Florence.)
68 The dance ritual Mukabele, 'coming face to face', of the Mevlevi order of Dervishes. (Watercolour, Turkish.)
69 Egyptian funeral procession with dancers and musicians. (Tomb of Khai, Saqqara, 18th or 19th dynasty, *c.* 1559–1200 BC, Cairo Museum.)

67

68

69

The sacred vessel as the body of the god is always under the special supervision of the priestess. It is the cauldron of incarnation, birth and rebirth. In Greek myth both Pelops and Dionysus became whole and perfect after having been 'cooked' in a magical cauldron of transformation. On this transformation fertility and light depend (70, 71). In Christian teaching death is conquered by death, which entails the voluntary self-sacrifice of the incarnate deity, and which becomes the cause of death releasing life (72, 73).

70 Medea and the ram. (Amphora, painted terracotta, Attica, 6th c. BC.)
71 Medea and the ram. (Hydria, painted terracotta, Vulci, 480–470 BC, British Museum, London.)
72 Christ at the Last Supper. (Detail of fresco by Leonardo da Vinci, S. Maria delle Grazie, Milan, *c.* 1495–97.)
73 Christ resurrected. (Detail of icon, Russia, *c.* 1700, National-museum, Stockholm.)

72

73

74

The body as the vessel of the spirit

In playing their part in the cosmic dance, all creatures are bound together by an intricate web of life. By his nature, man too participates in all cosmic events and is inwardly and outwardly interwoven with them. Increasingly, he becomes aware of the mutual dependency whereby influences pass between the universe and man's body. Being at all times intent on an intensification of life, the encounter with his inner self is experienced by him as life with greater depth and richness. On the way to himself he has recognized that the whole world is contained in himself, and that the divine revelation, which comes through him, the subjective medium, is formed and coloured in this process of manifestation. As the measure of all things and as the place of encounter of gods and demons, man is at all times his own most decisive adventure and experience. The universe, which he once peopled with countless divinities, is now rediscovered, moving within man himself.

The primary reality for man still is the reality of the psyche. Achieving the centre, however, presupposes the sacrifice of individual personality and of position in finite space, which makes possible the awareness that grace may be found anywhere. The body is the sacred vessel of the divinity, its veil or mask; yet at the same time it is the vehicle for its revelation. It is given dynamic emphasis by being painted (74), veiled or masked (75,

75

76